SACRAMENTS IN A SYNODAL CHURCH

SACRAMENTS
in a SYNODAL
CHURCH

Noel O'Sullivan

Published 2023 by
Veritas Publications
7–8 Lower Abbey Street
Dublin 1, Ireland
publications@veritas.ie
www.veritas.ie

ISBN 978 1 80097 061 8

10 9 8 7 6 5 4 3 2 1

All biblical quotations are taken from *The Holy Bible: New Revised Standard Version*, London: Darton, Longman & Todd, 2005, unless otherwise stated.

A catalogue record for this book is available from the British Library.

Designed by Clare Meredith, Veritas Publications
Printed in Ireland by SPRINT-print Ltd, Dublin

Veritas Publications is a member of Publishing Ireland.

Veritas books are printed on paper made from the wood pulp of managed forests. For every tree felled, at least one tree is planted, thereby renewing natural resources.

This book is dedicated to the students of St Patrick's Pontifical University, Maynooth, whose engagement with the author's modules on sacraments has greatly enriched this publication.

The author sincerely thanks the Maynooth Scholastic Trust for their financial support for this book.

CONTENTS

The Sixteen Documents of the Second Vatican Council.................. 9

Foreword
Dermot Farrell, Archbishop of Dublin.. 11

Introduction 15

Chapter One
The Source and Goal of Sacraments... 23

Chapter Two
How Did the Sacraments Develop? 39

Chapter Three
Sacraments of Christian Initiation I: Baptism and Confirmation 51

Chapter Four
Sacraments of Christian Initiation II: The Eucharist 67

Chapter Five
Sacraments of Healing and Wholeness 87

Chapter Six
The Sacrament of Marriage: Secular Reality and Saving Mystery..... 99

Chapter Seven
The Sacrament of Priesthood.. 113

General Conclusion
The Mission of the Synodal Church... 137

Bibliography.. 143

THE SIXTEEN DOCUMENTS OF THE SECOND VATICAN COUNCIL

Constitutions
- *Dei Verbum* (Dogmatic Constitution on Divine Revelation)
- *Lumen Gentium* (Dogmatic Constitution on the Church)
- *Sacrosanctum Concilium* (Constitution on the Sacred Liturgy)
- *Gaudium et Spes* (Pastoral Constitution on the Church in the Modern World)

Declarations
- *Gravissimum Educationis* (Declaration on Christian Education)
- *Nostra Aetate* (Declaration on the Relations of the Church to Non-Christian Religions)
- *Dignitatis Humanae* (Declaration on Religious Liberty)

Decrees
- *Ad Gentes* (Decree on the Church's Missionary Activity)
- *Presbyterorum Ordinis* (Decree on the Ministry and Life of Priests)
- *Apostolicam Actuositatem* (Decree on the Apostolate of Lay People)
- *Optatam Totius* (Decree on Training of Priests)
- *Perfectae Caritatis* (Decree on the Up-to-date Renewal of the Religious Life)
- *Christus Dominus* (Decree on the Pastoral Office of the Bishops in the Church)
- *Unitatis Redintegratio* (Decree on Ecumenism)
- *Orientalium Ecclesiarum* (Decree on the Catholic Eastern Churches)
- *Inter Mirifica* (Decree on the Means of Social Communication)

FOREWORD

At the launch of the synodal journey for the Diocese of Rome in September 2021, Pope Francis said, 'Being a synodal Church means being a Church that is the sacrament of Christ's promise that the Spirit will always be with us.'[1] As the whole Church walks on the synodal pathway initiated by the Pope, it is important that we engage in theological and pastoral reflection on the sacramentality of the Church in the synodal context. In this book Fr Noel O'Sullivan draws from the insight of the Second Vatican Council's Constitution on the Church, *Lumen Gentium*, into the Church as the 'universal sacrament of salvation' that ministers the seven sacraments.[2] I welcome its publication as it is a timely exposition of the role of the sacraments in the synodal journey and of the place of the synodal pathway in our understanding of the sacraments.

As we walk this synodal path, accompanied by the Holy Spirit, we engage in deep listening to the Word of God and to each other. We are strengthened on this journey by the sacraments of the Church but also challenged to celebrate them consciously and well, and to be missionary disciples, welcoming others into this dynamic communion of God's love. In the course of the book, the author takes an honest look at the landscape of Catholic practice in Ireland. He opens a discussion on how to engage those who might no longer see the sacraments as essential encounters with God's action. He grapples too with the impact on the Church of the Covid-19 restrictions of the early 2020s and their aftermath.

The author situates the sacraments in their Christological and ecclesial contexts, while exploring the role of synodality in their development and continued celebration. The joys and challenges of pastoral ministry are never far beneath the surface, informing the theological explorations. Throughout, he draws from the documents of the Second Vatican Council. He takes the incarnation as a starting point, when the Son of God came to journey together with us. In his homily for the opening of the synodal path in St Peter's Basilica in October 2021, Pope Francis said that 'participating in a Synod means placing ourselves on the same path as the Word made flesh' and highlighted our call 'to become experts in the *art of encounter*'.[3] Encounter with the person of Jesus must be at the centre of what we are and what we do, and the Church, realising the potential of synodality, must accompany people towards this encounter. Through prayer and discernment, we must make the new Spirit-inspired decisions needed to open up this encounter. The author savours the encounters that a spirituality of communion opens up to us. The incarnation opened up an encounter between God and humanity that has passed over into the sacraments as we journey together towards God's kingdom.

The encounter with Jesus in the sacraments is a profound source of strength for us. To quote Pope Francis again, in his apostolic letter on the liturgical formation of the people of God, issued in June 2022:

> In the Eucharist and in all the sacraments we are guaranteed the possibility of encountering the Lord Jesus and of having the power of his Paschal Mystery reach us. The salvific power of the sacrifice of Jesus, his every word, his every gesture, glance, and feeling reaches us through the celebration of the sacraments.[4]

Flowing from the understanding of the Church as the basic sacrament, the author's consideration of each of the sacraments can orient us on our synodal path. He finds inspiration for the synodal way ahead in the shared journey the Church has made thus far in understanding and living the sacraments. He shows how the Church travelled a path between discerning that Jesus instituted each of the seven sacraments and gradually determining its concrete celebration, and how this happened at different speeds for different sacraments.

Beginning with the sacraments of Christian initiation, we see baptism as our incorporation into this sacramental life of encounter with God and his Church, confirmation as our Pentecost and the Eucharist as the anticipation of our union in the life of the Trinity. The author calls the Eucharist the 'source and summit of synodality'. Writing about the sacraments of healing and wholeness, he explores our encounter with Christ, the healer of broken humanity. The call to conversion we hear in the Word of God culminates sacramentally in the sacrament of penance. That call to conversion is necessarily at the core of any pastoral strategy that will be shaped by the synodal process. We must persevere in humble commitment to right the wrongs of the past and make best practice in all areas of Church life a constant and permanent way of life. In the sacrament of the sick, we meet Christ the healer, who makes us whole again. In the sacraments of particular vocations, God provides for the fundamental relationships that bond us in communion. Jesus raised marriage to the level of a sacrament so that the man and the woman in their love can be a sign of Christ's relationship with his Church, his people.

On the synodal journey, it is important that there be a shared understanding of the relationship between the priesthood of the baptised and the ministerial priesthood, and this book highlights the rich possibilities inherent in this relationship. For the author, 'the priesthood of the baptised is the basis for a synodal Church'. He demonstrates a healthy complementarity between these sacramental continuations of the priesthood of Christ in the Church, how they are ordered to one another, as is highlighted in *Lumen Gentium*.[5] The ministerial priesthood is at the service of the priesthood of the baptised. The relationship has great potential for synodality among priests and parishioners in the parishes. There are implications here for priestly formation also, and the text contains an examination of conscience for clergy when it treats of human maturity.

In fact, a feature of the book is the author's ability to harmonise different theological approaches. He can see the metaphysical and symbolic approaches to the sacraments, when taken together, as enriching our understanding. He takes a similar approach to the Eucharist as sacrifice and memorial. His treatment of the sacraments is done with a genuine ecumenical sensitivity.

Returning to the words of Pope Francis to his own diocesan flock in Rome, the Pope pointed out that 'synodality is an expression of the

Church's nature, her form, style and mission' and recalled the teaching of *Lumen Gentium* that 'the Church, in Christ, is like a sacrament – a sign and instrument of communion with God and of the unity of the whole human race.'[6] From this, he drew a strong corollary:

> That sentence, which echoes the testimony of the Council of Jerusalem, contradicts those who would take God's place, presuming to shape the Church on the basis of their own cultural and historical convictions, forcing it to set up armed borders, toll booths, forms of spirituality that blaspheme the gratuitousness of God's involvement in our lives.[7]

We are in the early steps of this renewed consciousness of synodality initiated by Pope Francis. This book is a helpful resource for seeing beyond those armed borders and toll booths, so that our sacramental life may be a wellspring for participation in the Church, communion with Christ and with one another, and mission to all people.

✠ *Dermot Farrell*
Archbishop of Dublin

Notes

1   Pope Francis, *Address to the Faithful of the Diocese of Rome*, Paul VI Audience Hall, 18 September 2021.

2   Vatican II, *Lumen Gentium*, 1964, 48.

3   Pope Francis, *Homily for the Opening of the Synodal Path*, St Peter's Basilica, Rome, 10 October 2021.

4   Pope Francis, *Desiderio Desideravi*, 2022, 11.

5   *Lumen Gentium*, 10.

6   Pope Francis, *Address to the Faithful of the Diocese of Rome*, citing *Lumen Gentium*, 1.

7   Ibid.

INTRODUCTION

One of the main distinguishing marks of Christianity as understood and lived in the Roman Catholic tradition is its focus on sacraments. The sacraments play an explicit and pivotal role in the pastoral practice of parish life. It is through the sacraments of baptism, confirmation and the Eucharist that we enter the family of God, the Church. The forgiveness and healing of Christ are made available to us in a tangible way in the sacraments of penance and the anointing of the sick. The vocations of marriage and priesthood are made possible too by their specific sacraments. Using theological language, we can say that the sacraments are central to our ecclesiology and Christology. From both a pastoral and theological point of view we are constantly challenged to understand and integrate the sacraments into our Christian life. Edward Schillebeeckx OP (1914–2009) has cogently summed up the centrality of the sacraments:

> The sacraments are at the very heart of Christianity. They are the centre from which the Christian life stands out in relief. … Once the sacramental way of life is abandoned, Christianity itself and, in the long run, any kind of 'ecclesiality' [i.e. being Church] whatever will be lost.[1]

Several questions arise in relation to sacraments, especially as we make our way through a society marked by secularism and growing indifference to religion. The Catholic Church has a much-diminished place in modern culture, not least because of horrific scandals caused by some members of the Church. In addition, the 'crash' in vocations to priesthood in some countries has resulted in a scarcity of priests to celebrate the sacraments. The sacraments themselves are sometimes seen as near magical events whereby God is made present – the implication being that God is otherwise absent, which, of course, is not the case. The situation was exacerbated by the Covid-19 pandemic, when the celebration of the sacraments was not possible for long periods.

This is the background against which we must look afresh at the sacraments. For these reasons I believe in the need for a publication on the sacraments, aimed at a wide audience, that will take into account the complex range of issues involved. This book sets out to situate the sacraments in their Christological and ecclesial contexts in an attempt to liberate them from the mechanical and individualistic mentality that can be so undermining of them. The approach will be pastoral, but it will be informed by a theological method that has its roots in scripture and tradition and that takes account of current thinking. Of central importance in that regard is synodality. Pope Francis has called for a radical reappraisal of how we live as Church, one that acknowledges that we travel the Way together.

SYNODAL SIGNPOSTS

The term 'synodality' owes its origin to two Greek terms, *sun* (with) and *hé hodos* (the road/journey): we journey on the one road together. The basis of synodality is the incarnation: the Son of God became one of us and joined us on the journey of life, with its joys and sorrows, until he met with a most brutal death. And he continues to journey with us: 'And remember, I am with you always, to the end of the age' (Mt 28:20). We too need to journey together. Though we have different functions in the Church and different vocations, nonetheless, we are all travelling together. The Church is a body, as St Paul highlights (1 Cor 12:12-27), but she must give a place to each of her members: the inarticulate, the poor and those in precarious situations. As the preparatory document for the 2021–4 synod affirms:

> [I]t will be of fundamental importance that the voice of the poor and excluded also find a place, not only that of those who have some role or responsibility within the particular Churches.[2]

16

Synodality is not a new pastoral experiment that gives a platform to the theologically articulate; it is a constitutive dimension of the Church and always has been. St John Chrysostom (*c.*347–407) stated that 'Church and Synod are synonymous'.[3]

In *Evangelii Gaudium* ('The Joy of the Gospel'), Pope Francis proposes a 'mystique' of living together that can be transposed to synodality:

> Today, … we sense the challenge of finding and sharing a 'mystique' of living together, of mingling and encounter, of embracing and supporting one another, of stepping into this flood tide which, while chaotic, can become a genuine experience of fraternity, a caravan of solidarity, a sacred pilgrimage.[4]

We can also speak of the 'mystique' of travelling together, a 'mystique' of synodality.

For too long in the Church we have drawn false distinctions between the laity and clergy, between priests, bishops and popes. As we have different functions, we presumed that we were on different roads: the Pope and bishops were on the high road, priests and religious were on another road and the laity were at the bottom on a dirt track. Pope Francis' call for synodality is a recognition that we all need to journey together. Ordination does not give people a greater degree of holiness. All are called to the highest degree of holiness. One idea that should be important as we move towards a synod at local and universal levels in the Church is the rediscovery of the priesthood of the baptised. This is not just a new idea that comes from Vatican II; it was there from the beginning but has lain dormant. It is mentioned in the First Letter of St Peter:

> But you are a chosen race, a royal priesthood, a holy nation, God's own people, in order that you may proclaim the mighty acts of him who called you out of darkness into his marvellous light. (1 Pt 2:9)

In our chapter on priesthood we will examine in detail the meaning and implications of the priesthood of all the baptised.

Pope Francis has proposed three pillars of synodality: communion, participation and mission. I like to think of these as synodal signposts: they indicate the way forward. I also suggest that they are three eucharistic terms: communion, participation and mission. Pope John Paul II describes eucharistic communion as bringing about 'in a sublime way the mutual "abiding" of Christ in each of his followers: "Abide in me, and I in you" (Jn 15:4)'.[5] Communion with one another and with Christ is a core principle of synodality. In our chapter on the Eucharist we will focus in more detail on the relationship between synodality and the Eucharist. From *Sacrosanctum Concilium*, the Vatican II document on the liturgy, we get the phrase 'full and active participation'.[6] It is also an aspiration of the synodal ideal. And then there is mission. In his first encyclical Pope Francis has called us all to be 'missionary disciples':

> I dream of a 'missionary option', that is, a missionary impulse capable of transforming everything, so that the Church's customs, ways of doing things, times and schedules, language and structures can be suitably channelled for the evangelisation of today's world rather than for her self-preservation.[7]

WHAT TO EXPECT

It is a privilege and a challenge to write a book on any aspect of the Christian life. What gives the impetus to this book on the sacraments is the urgent need to recognise the centrality of the idea of sacrament in Christianity and to explore the richness of each of the seven sacraments. The term 'sacrament' is often misunderstood, and it is isolated from Christ and his Church. For this reason, the first chapter lays the foundations. It treats of Christ as sacrament and proposes that the Church is the sacrament of Christ. The term 'sacrament' itself needs to be unveiled. A sacrament is a ritual with materials and words in which Christ is actively present for the benefit of a particular individual or group. Sometimes it is Christ the healer and reconciler. On other occasions Christ is present to give his Spirit so that an individual may become part of his life in the Church (baptism) or become his witness (confirmation). Then again, the ritual may change someone to become his representative as a successor of the apostles (bishops) and others to represent them (priests). But Christ's presence in the Eucharist is different from what it is in the other sacraments. The material on the altar at Mass is changed into Christ himself: it is no longer bread and wine. That existential presence is different from Christ's engagement in the other six sacraments. The Eucharist is regarded as the source and summit of the other sacraments. We see immediately that we cannot treat individual sacraments in isolation from each other and, more importantly, from the Mass. We need to be aware of their relationship with one another.

The second chapter explores the history of the sacraments from their roots in the words and actions of Christ to the recognition of the seven sacraments at the Council of Florence in 1439. We follow the debates as to the number of sacraments, which took more than a millennium to finalise. The sacraments of baptism and the Eucharist were quickly recognised but the recognition of marriage as a sacrament was very late indeed. For this reason, the churches that emerged from the Reformation usually accept just baptism and the Eucharist as sacraments. An important concept that arises in this context is that of the institution of the sacraments by Christ. The Church teaches that Christ instituted the seven sacraments, and we will explore what this means in this chapter.

Our third chapter treats of the first two sacraments of initiation: baptism and confirmation. It seems that these were originally part of the one rite and that this rite eventually emerged as two sacraments. We trace the biblical origins of these sacraments, relying on the Acts of the Apostles. We look at baptism from the perspective of the initiation of adults rather than infants as this enables us to understand better what baptism means. We do so through the lens of the Rite of Christian Initiation of Adults (RCIA) programme. We recommend strongly that the parish community, together with its priests, needs to discuss how best to prepare children and adults for the sacraments of initiation. The parish needs to complement what is being done in the schools in that regard. Courses need to be provided for the parents of children being presented for the sacraments. These courses can be given by parishioners who have been trained to do so. In this way we avoid a mechanical approach to the sacraments whereby they are reduced to mere cultural rites of passage. In the case of smaller parishes, the courses can be the work of a number of parishes together. This too is an exercise in synodality.

The sacraments of initiation reach their completion in the Eucharist, which is the subject of chapter 4. Our approach here is to trace the connection between the Last Supper and the Eucharist, recognising that the death and resurrection of Christ is anticipated in the Last Supper and remembered in our Mass with the full import of the meaning of remembrance in the Jewish mind. While it is Christ who is present in the consecrated bread and wine, the Father and the Holy Spirit are part of the mystery being celebrated. The eucharistic prayer is addressed to the Father, and the Holy Spirit comes upon the elements transforming them into Christ's body and blood (the *epiclesis*). The term 'sacrifice' is often misunderstood as the appeasing of an angry God. We unveil the fuller meaning of the term and explore the link between sacrifice and communion. A detailed analysis of the four institution narratives opens up the richness of the mystery.[8] The connection between liturgy and life leads to an awareness of the practical consequences of participation in the Eucharist. In each celebration of the Mass something of the end time is present: the kingdom in its fullness is anticipated.

Given the focus of this book on synodality, we take the opportunity in our chapter on the Eucharist to show the connection between the Eucharist and synodality, illustrating the immediacy of the three synodal signposts, i.e. communion, participation and mission, to both realities, the Eucharist being the source and summit of synodality.

Chapter 5 – 'Sacraments of Healing and Wholeness' – brings together the sacrament of penance and the sacrament of the sick. We expose their biblical roots, with particular emphasis on the ministry of forgiveness and healing exercised by Christ. As with all the sacraments, it is important to see their connection with one another. These two sacraments are easily linked to baptism. One way of expressing the link is to see them as supports for baptism. In the cut and thrust of life in the world, what we became at baptism can be damaged. One way of expressing this is through the biblical terms 'image' and 'likeness'. According to the Fathers of the Church we never lose the image of God; however, likeness grows in the economy of salvation, and it can be diminished or lost. These sacraments help to recover the likeness of God in us. But it is the Eucharist above all that is the food of the Christian life.

The sacrament of penance is most likely reaping the whirlwind resulting from an excessive juridical approach in the past, which led some people to fear the 'confession box' and to become afflicted with scruples. Inspired by Vatican II's *Sacrosanctum Concilium*, there has been considerable reform of the sacrament to ensure that it is more holistic and better contributes to the conversion of the penitent. Healing love rather than fear is uppermost in the way in which the sacrament is celebrated now. The social dimension of sin and forgiveness is given its rightful place, helped especially by the different forms of the sacrament today.

The sacrament of the sick is closely connected to that of penance because it too involves the forgiveness of sin. It is no longer just a sacrament for the dying but is offered also to those who are seriously ill. Its emphasis is on holistic healing and not just the healing of physical illness. The aim of both these sacraments is closer union with God and, as a result, a fuller human life, which is a life of love for one another.

The sacrament of marriage was the last of the sacraments to be recognised as such. The challenges encountered in its regard for over a thousand years are the subject of chapter 6. We trace the history of marriage from pre-Christian times, revealing that marriage is a creaturely reality and does not have an explicit religious provenance. This understanding has positive consequences because it recognises the goodness of human nature. It shows that the secular can be a vehicle for the divine. The history of marriage in the pagan religions of Rome and Greece reveals how the most intimate human relationship seeks a religious expression. Furthermore, the story of Christian marriage shows it to be a secular reality and only gradually does its full religious import become explicit. The Old Testament invoked the marriage relationship as a symbol of God's love for humanity. In the New Testament it is seen as expressive of Christ's relationship with the Church. Several centuries later marriage is recognised as a cause of grace and, therefore, a sacrament in its own right. In the Western Church we still believe it is the couple who are the ministers of the sacrament of marriage, though in the East the priest is regarded as the minister.

The priesthood is treated in chapter 7. Here we give an exposition of three priesthoods: Christ the priest, the priesthood of the baptised and the ministerial priest. We establish the evidence for understanding Christ as a priest, though the evidence for it in scripture is limited. The main scriptural source is the Letter to the Hebrews 4:14–10:18. We then put in place convincing arguments for seeing all the baptised as priests, not in the same sense as the ministerial priest, obviously, but in a real sense nonetheless. The priesthood of the baptised is the basis for a synodal Church. All the faithful share equally in the communion that is Church. This is a privilege and responsibility. The laity should never be regarded as 'consumers' of grace 'distributed' by priests. All are called to participate fully in the Eucharist and in the life of the Church. The emphasis by Pope Francis on synodality is an opportunity to rediscover what has always been believed but too infrequently practised.

We trace the development of specialised ministry from earliest times. We do not subscribe to the view that Jesus ordained twelve bishops at the Last Supper and that they, in turn, ordained priests and deacons. The threefold structure of orders (bishop, priest and deacon) that we have today developed gradually from a myriad of ministries. Our seventh chapter ends with an exposition of the permanent diaconate.

The general conclusion highlights some of the new insights that have been developed in the book, especially when viewed through the lens of synodality. We will take a final look here at our synodal signposts and give particular attention to mission.

Notes

1   Edward Schillebeeckx, *Christ the Sacrament of the Encounter with God*, London: Sheed and Ward, 1963 [Dutch orig.: *Christus, Sacrament van de Godsontmoeting*, Bilthoven: H. Nelissen, 1960], p. 212.

2   Synod of Bishops, *For a Synodal Church: Communion, Participation, and Mission – Synod 2021–2023 Preparatory Document*, Vatican: Libreria Editrice Vaticana, 2021, 31, p. 38.

3   St John Chrysostom, *Commentary on Psalm 149*, quoted in Synod of Bishops, *Preparatory Document*, 11, p. 14.

4   Pope Francis, *Evangelii Gaudium*, 2013, 87.

5   Pope John Paul II, *Ecclesia de Eucharistia*, 2003, 22.

6   Vatican II, *Sacrosanctum Concilium*, 1963, 14.

7   Pope Francis, *Evangelii Gaudium*, 27.

8   The four accounts of the institution of the Eucharist at the Last Supper are: 1 Corinthians 11:23-6; Luke 22:19-20; Mark 14:22-4; and Matthew 26:26-8.

CHAPTER ONE

THE SOURCE AND GOAL OF SACRAMENTS

PASTORAL PRACTICE: CRISIS AND OPPORTUNITY

Once a baby is born most parents think about booking a date for the baptism. Irrespective of their normal faith practice, most families want their baby christened. Similarly, parents will insist that their child receives Holy Communion. This is regarded as a major milestone in the life of the child and of the family. Even when parents have chosen to send their child to a non-Catholic school, they will do all in their power to ensure that first Communion is still possible. Likewise with confirmation: most children in Catholic primary schools are put forward for this sacrament even though many of them haven't been inside the doors of a church since their first Communion. Schools like to showcase their wares, and many of them see the sacraments as opportune occasions to do so. Not all are so utilitarian, of course. Generally, the children themselves are believing if they have been taught well in school. When this is backed up in the home, these sacraments are genuine celebrations of Christian faith and life. But the common experience on the ground is that even the best schools cannot make up for the lack of faith and practice in the family.

This socio-cultural pattern, common to many parishes, is a major cause for concern. The sacraments of initiation are being reduced to secular rites of passage. The temptation to despondency is obvious: priests and teachers are discouraged when they see the wonderful display at the Saturday first Communion followed on the Sunday by a mere handful of those same children at Mass. Priests too can become enablers of this pattern. There needs to be a proper preparation for each sacrament. It is not sufficient to have a set time for baptisms and not even know how many families will present their child for baptism. I remember on one occasion visiting a priest and he apologised that he couldn't offer me a cup of tea because it was near the time for baptisms. I asked how many were expected and he replied, 'However many turn up; they know the time when we have baptisms.' That scenario leads to a vicious circle whereby priests undermine the sacrament by treating it casually.

Without being alarmist, we can talk of a crisis in relation to the sacraments. If this crisis can be seen as an opportunity for a new evangelisation then all is not lost. The etymology of the term 'crisis' suggests as much: 'crisis' means 'to decide', 'to make a choice'. We are living in an exciting time in the Church. The challenge is to turn the crisis into the opportunity that it is. We need to look at ways whereby the demand for the sacraments of initiation on the part of parents can become an opportunity to re-evangelise those parents and families. This alternative is evident in some parishes where courses are offered to parents in advance of the sacraments of initiation to promote reflection on the real meaning of the sacraments. The inappropriateness of putting a child forward for a sacrament that will be an isolated event with no religious follow-up is made clear. That is a disservice to the child and can be most confusing. In my experience, parents are quite willing to come to these courses, which are usually delivered by trained parishioners. This is an example of synodality. It is neither feasible nor appropriate that preparation for sacraments be done by the priest alone. It is not feasible because of the lack of priests but, in any case, it is not appropriate given that the baptised share in the priesthood of Christ. These parents can make a radical difference to the way parishes function and in this way the sacraments can become life-giving rather than just cultural rites of passage.

Proper catechesis should also precede the reception of the sacraments. Pope Paul VI, in his apostolic exhortation *Evangelii Nuntiandi*, highlights the importance of the faith preparation necessary for a proper celebration of sacraments:

The role of evangelisation is precisely to educate people in the faith in such a way as to lead each individual Christian to live the sacraments as true sacraments of faith – and not to receive them passively or reluctantly.[1]

THE THEOLOGICAL ISSUES

Best pastoral practice needs to be informed by a thorough knowledge of the meaning of sacramentality and the history of its development in the Church. Of all the areas of theology, the gestation of the sacraments took an exceptionally long time, the number of sacraments being settled definitively as seven as late as the fifteenth century at the Council of Florence, with the bull *Exultate Deo*, promulgated on 22 November 1439.[2] But there are current theological questions around the meaning of sacraments. Two schools of theological thinking dominate the issue: the metaphysical and the symbolic.

The metaphysical (*meta* meaning 'beyond') tradition highlights the sacraments as *causes* of grace. Understanding the sacraments from a metaphysical perspective goes back to St Augustine's (354–430) Platonist position, through to the Aristotelian conceptual framework of St Thomas Aquinas (1225–74). It became critically important at the time of the Reformation to affirm that sacraments cause grace because the Reformers denied that this was the case. In using the categories of metaphysics, the theological tradition was expressing its understanding of sacraments in language and concepts that had currency in the contemporary world. Theology always attempts to speak to the culture of its time; otherwise, it is talking to itself.

The second approach to sacraments, which developed in the twentieth century, is symbolism. Symbolism is influenced by currents of thought in linguistics and modern philosophy. Karl Rahner SJ (1904–84), Louis-Marie Chauvet (b.1942) and Herbert Vorgrimler (1929–2014) have been prominent among theologians who regard the symbolic as central to our understanding of sacraments. Their basic thesis is that all reality is symbolic, including the human being. Rahner talks about the human person as being real in the fundamental symbol of their body. Pope Francis too highlights the symbolic nature of the body: 'Our body is a symbol because it is an intimate union of soul and body; it is the visibility of the spiritual soul in the corporeal order'.[3] This is how Herbert Vorgrimler sums up the symbolic approach to sacraments:

> If all human reality is symbolic reality, this is certainly true of the relationship God has willed to establish with human beings, and that decisively shapes human reality from beginning to end. If God desires to be present to human beings, God's presence must create a symbolic expression for itself in order that it can be 'real' for human beings, since the complete disparity between God and the human makes an unmediated presence and communication of God impossible.[4]

The metaphysical approach, as the name implies, tells us what is happening beyond the physical, that is, beyond what can be seen and felt at the human level, namely that grace is imparted. The symbolic approach makes a tangible connection between the material, human level and the spiritual level. Throughout this book we will become familiar with these two approaches to sacramentality. Our thesis is that they are not mutually exclusive, but rather that, taken together, they can enrich our understanding of the way God gives himself to humanity in the sacraments.

ANTHROPOLOGICAL UNDERPINNING

So where do we begin? Where is the starting point for a theology of the sacraments? It must begin with creation or, more precisely, anthropology. The nature of the human being is such as to need rites to plumb the depths of who each person is. Because life is a mystery, its meaning and comprehension are elusive. Certain experiences awaken us to who we are, like the birth of a child, the death of a parent or spouse, the experience of love or the fact of living in community or society. Vorgrimler puts it like this:

> Undoubtedly there are events in individual and community life that disturb and fascinate us (such things as being born, common meals, sexuality, death) and therefore incline people to surround them with rites, and in this way to pay attention

to the deeper dimensions of their being and to give heed to the presence of God.[5]

Anthropologists tell us that something corresponding in our terminology to an altar and a priest has been found in all societies and tribes investigated. The human being is ritualistic by nature. Regularly, we see poignant scenes of love and grief where accidents and other tragic deaths have taken place, for example flowers and messages piled high at the site of a tragedy. All these instances are evidence that the human person needs ritual to express relationship and feeling at the deepest level.

In the Old Testament we find that the sacraments are prefigured in several ways. Circumcision is evocative of baptism. The sacrifice of the paschal lamb is the highpoint of Jewish religious life and anticipates Christ, the Lamb of God.

In the healing miracles of Jesus, we find human, tangible signs of his power. These may be considered as prefiguring sacraments. The healing of a leper, recorded in all three Synoptic Gospels (Mt 8:1-4; Mk 1:40-5; Lk 5:12-16), shows Jesus stretching out his hand and touching the leper: 'And immediately the leprosy left him' (Lk 5:13). Jesus heals two blind men in Matthew's gospel: 'Then he touched their eyes, saying "According to your faith be it done to you"' (Mt 9:27-31; see also Mt 20:29-34). Touching the hem of his garment is sufficient for several people to be cured (Mt 14:34-6; Mk 6:53-6). A more elaborate sacramental prefiguring is found in chapter 9 of St John's gospel. Healing the man born blind (Jn 9:1-8), Jesus makes a paste with spittle and tells the man to wash in the pool of Siloam. When that ritual is complete the man returns with full sight. Of course, Jesus also performs miracles without signs of this kind. For example, when healing Bartimaeus, the blind beggar, Jesus simply says to him: 'Go; your faith has made you well' (Mk 10:46-52). Jesus doesn't need ritual signs to make a miracle possible. It is we who need the tangible sign of his presence and power.

Through the sacraments, material creation is employed in the work of salvation. Natural substances – water, oil, bread, wine, etc. – have become the symbols and vehicles of grace. This is a far cry from the different philosophies that regard creation as evil, for example Manichaeism, Gnosticism, Catharism and Albigensianism. We will see later in our chapter on marriage how these negative attitudes to

27

creation and human nature were counteracted. Defining marriage as a sacrament was, and is, a most significant signal that the human can be the vehicle of the divine. In the case of marriage, the partners are the instruments of grace to one another.

CHRISTOLOGICAL AND ECCLESIAL FOUNDATION OF THE SACRAMENTS

First of all, we will examine the incarnational and ecclesial basis of sacraments. The principal way in which God is present to the world is sacramentally. That follows from the law of the incarnation. Human, tangible things are part of the mediation of God to humanity. As Jean-Philippe Revel (1931–2013) puts it: 'The divine life is given to us through the mediation of this world's realities. It [the divine life] is involved in our human life in the most concrete way.'[6] The human and the divine are not incompatible. While the definitive revelation of God took place in the person of Jesus Christ, he is now accessed in the Church, which is his body. Some theologians speak of the Church as the continuation of the incarnation, for example Yves Congar OP (1904–95). Pope St Leo the Great (who served as pope from 440–61), the theological architect of the Council of Chalcedon (451), has given us this authoritative dictum: 'The visible presence of our Redeemer passed over into sacraments.'[7] Pope Francis teases out the implications of that statement in his apostolic letter *Desiderio Desideravi*. He comments as follows:

> From the very beginning the Church had grasped, enlightened by the Holy Spirit, that that which was visible in Jesus, that which could be seen with the eyes and touched with the hands, his words and his gestures, the concreteness of the incarnate Word – everything of Him had passed into the celebration of the sacraments.[8]

The Church is the locus of God's presence, especially through its sacramental activity. Here we will take as our starting point a presentation of the theology of sacraments, or sacramental theology. This will situate the sacraments in their proper community and ecclesial context.

The sacraments are not isolated rituals; they are not just personal experiences between the individual and God. The sacraments are part of the life and liturgy of the Church and cannot be understood apart from the Church. Referring to the Church, in turn, presumes an understanding of Christ and the incarnation. So, the point of departure for a consideration of the Christian sacraments is an exploration of the meaning of the incarnation followed by a consideration of the theology of the Church (ecclesiology). Only then can we be confident that the sacraments are not reduced to isolated rituals. More specifically, our focus needs to be Christ as the revelation of the Father or, more accurately, the revelation of the Trinity. Christ came to show us God's love in a definitive way. He not only shows us that love; he is God's love in person. For this reason, we can speak of Christ as the sacrament of God. We will return to this idea presently. First, however, we need to make some preliminary remarks about the incarnation of Christ.

The coming of Christ (the Messiah) was anticipated in the Old Testament. So many texts – especially when we read them retrospectively – hint at the coming of the Messiah. We think in particular of Isaiah and Zephaniah. Yet the incarnation happened in history in a way that could never have been foreseen. God did not become man in some evolutionary manner; he burst into history in a way that could never have been anticipated. Continuity and rupture marked the coming of Christ. It is important to underscore that the incarnation is not the summit of a process that had been taking place in history in a Hegelian way, i.e. that the incarnation was a natural development within history and not the dramatic intervention of God in history. This erroneous interpretation would mean that the incarnation was merely a stage in an evolutionary world view. Rather, the incarnation comes directly from God through the intermediary role of Mary. This will have important consequences for how we understand the Church and the sacraments.

Karl Rahner makes three distinctions in relation to the term 'sacrament': the *Ursakrament* is the original or primordial sacrament of God and refers to Christ; the *Grundsakrament,* or foundational sacrament, is the Church; and *Sakrament* refers to the seven sacraments. Rahner helped to lift the sacraments from being isolated acts and situated them within the foundational sacrament of the Church, which is founded on the primordial sacrament, Christ.[9]

Rahner's definition of the individual sacraments incorporates an ecclesial context for them:

> The sacraments make concrete and actual, for the life of the individual, the symbolic reality of the Church as the primary sacrament and therefore constitute at once, in keeping with the nature of this Church, a symbolic reality.[10]

By 'symbolic reality' Rahner means that what is symbolised is present in the symbol. The symbol is not referring to something absent. Vorgrimler expresses this idea very clearly:

> As a community of believing human beings who desire to follow Jesus, the Church has an external, visible dimension that points to something deeper. Its inner dimension is constituted by the fact that Jesus Christ, in the Holy Spirit, makes it his sign and instrument, which he uses in order to carry out his work of renewing and reshaping humanity, to the glory of his Father. The external dimension is thus like an historically and communally structured sign that does not point to a foreign, absent entity, but to one who is present, one who is the real agent of the whole.[11]

To say that the Church is the sacrament of Christ means that Christ is present and active in the Church. Individual sacraments are then the actualisation of the Church as sacrament in a given situation. Rahner again summarises: 'A sacrament is present when an *essential* self-actualisation of the church becomes effective in a concrete and decisive situation in some person's life.'[12]

CHRIST: SYMBOL OF REVELATION/SACRAMENT OF GOD

'Jesus Christ is the Mediator and at the same time the fullness of revelation.'[13] Revelation can be described as symbolic communication. However, a difficulty arises: if Jesus is the symbol of God, does this mean that he is only human and merely represents God who is totally other? At this point we need to home in on our understanding of symbol. Karl Rahner distinguishes between two types of symbol. The common use of symbol is 'representative', in that it is a sign that represents something or someone who is absent. A flag can be a symbol of a country; a photograph can represent a person or thing. There is another way of understanding symbol, however. Rahner proposes the idea of a 'realising' symbol. In this sense a symbol can indicate the presence of what is symbolised. Schillebeeckx calls this a 'real' symbol. Rahner describes symbol in this sense as follows:

> The symbol is the reality, constituted by the thing symbolised as an inner moment of itself, which reveals and proclaims the thing symbolised, and is itself full of the thing symbolised, being its concrete form of existence.[14]

Christ is the symbol of God par excellence, with symbol understood in its second sense: Christ is a 'realising' symbol of God. An evocative example of Christ as the realising symbol of God is the consecrated host in the monstrance at eucharistic adoration. The host is not a representative symbol, i.e., a sign of Christ who is elsewhere. No, in the monstrance what we see is a host, but this host has already been consecrated at Mass and is Christ himself. When we say that Christ is the fullness of revelation, we mean that he is the symbol of God, understood in the sense that God is present in him; he is God. Avery Dulles SJ (1918–2008) writes: 'The man Jesus Christ is both the symbol and the incarnation of the eternal Logos, who communicates himself by becoming fully human without ceasing to be divine.'[15] In sacramental theology Christ is described as the sacrament of God. By that we mean that God is present in him effecting grace and salvation. In the context of revelation, it is more appropriate to speak of Christ as symbol rather than as sacrament. Both terms complement each other, however.

CHURCH AS SACRAMENT OF CHRIST

Seeing the Church as the locus of the sacraments as we know them is an obvious point. What needs some attention is the idea that the Church is the foundational sacrament (*Grundsakrament*). To what extent then can we describe the Church as sacrament? To answer that question, we will turn to the Vatican II document on the Church, *Lumen Gentium*, and explore the idea in the writings of Henri de Lubac SJ (1896–1991), one of the architects of Vatican II.

First of all, we must take up the issue of the blossoming of the idea of the Church as sacrament in the Second Vatican Council. The document *Lumen Gentium*, from its first paragraph, refers to the Church as the sacrament of Christ. In paragraph 48 the emphasis is on the work of the Spirit, sent by Christ to set up his Body:

> Christ, lifted up from the earth, has drawn all people to himself. Rising from the dead he sent his life-giving Spirit upon his disciples and through him set up his Body which is the Church *as* the universal sacrament of salvation.[16]

It is clear from these examples that the Vatican document understands the Church as the sacrament of Christ, but not in the same sense as the other sacraments. 'Sacrament' in terms of the Church is used analogically; the Church is 'like' a sacrament. This reserve in *Lumen Gentium* avoids the danger of seeing the Church as an eighth sacrament. It also has important implications for ecumenical dialogue, with some Protestant communions being sensitive to the idea of the Church as an intermediary between God and humanity. The proposal of the Church as being 'in the nature of a sacrament' remains a prudent legacy of the Vatican Council.[17]

We now turn to Henri de Lubac. De Lubac's designation of the Church as the sacrament of Christ – though not a new idea – was innovative when he proposed it in 1938 and prefigured the Vatican Council document *Lumen Gentium*. St Cyprian of Carthage (*c.*200–*c.*258) used the phrase *inseparabile unitatis sacramentum* ('the inseparable sacrament of unity') in reference to the Church.[18] We will refer to two instances of the idea of the Church as the sacrament of Christ in the works of de Lubac. In his first published work, *Catholicism*, he writes:

> If Christ is the sacrament of God, the Church is for us the sacrament of Christ; she represents him, in the full and ancient meaning of the term; she really makes him present. She not only carries on his work, but she is his very continuation.[19]

Just as Christ became incarnate in a human body he is now present in his Body, the Church. Through the incarnation God is not only made known but is present in the world. In that sense Christ is the sacrament of God. To say that the Church is the sacrament of Christ is to claim that his incarnation, his life, his death and his resurrection are present in the Church. It is not just that his effects are there; it is more than that. This is never clearer than in the Eucharist: there it is as if we are standing on Calvary or sitting at the Last Supper, and, like Mary Magdalen, we meet Christ in the garden of resurrection. These events are not repeated, but they are present.

The totalising emphasis given in the quotation above by de Lubac to the function of the Church in regard to the sacraments avoids the individualistic approach to these seven moments of grace that has so marked pastoral practice, where the sacraments were sometimes seen as moments of personal devotion between the individual soul and Christ. In this regard de Lubac recalls the social aspect of the sacraments, affirming that 'it is through his union with the community that the Christian is united to Christ'.[20] This has always been the tradition of the Church but has been all too frequently ignored. De Lubac gives the pertinent example of the sacrament of penance as a cogent expression of what this means in practice. In the early Church the practice of public penance and pardon was a striking way of highlighting that the reconciliation of the sinner is first of all a reconciliation with the Church, this being an efficacious sign of their reconciliation with God. That reality is still maintained through the intermediary role of the priest in the sacrament of penance.[21]

In proposing the parallel between Christ as the sacrament of God and the Church as the sacrament of Christ, de Lubac is highlighting the continuity between the incarnation and the Church. His understanding of 'sacrament' deserves some summary attention. A sacrament is both a sign of union between God and humanity and the means to that union. As we have seen, a sign in the sacramental sense is not an intermediary between two realities, one referring to the other. Rather, the sign is the mediation of the new reality. In terms of the Church, she is the locus and means of the mediation of union between God and humanity. The Church is not the mediator but the mediation. The Church is not Christ; she is the sacrament of Christ.

De Lubac emphasises that a sacramental sign is not provisional, not one that can be discarded. For example, we are not free to exchange the bread and wine for some other symbols. Applied to the Church, this has important pastoral as well as theological implications. De Lubac is aware of the tendency in certain quarters to see the Church as a disposable burden that, if discarded, would open more ready access to God. What he says in this regard is even more pertinent seventy years after it was first penned:

> One who gives way to the temptations of a false spiritualisation and wants to shake off the Church as a burdensome yoke or set her aside as a cumbersome intermediary will soon find himself embracing the void or end up by worshipping false gods.[22]

This warning finds an echo in the aberration of individualism that so marked certain expressions of Christianity, and which preoccupied de Lubac from his very first work. For de Lubac, the Church is not a federation of like-minded Christians who happen to have opted to worship together and to live in a certain way. De Lubac asserts that the first Christians did not create the Church by their arrival:

> The Church is not a result; at least she is not a mere result, the simple fruit of a confluence. She has not been formed by individuals who, having believed in Jesus Christ each on his own part and each in his own way, decided to join together in order to organise their belief and their life in common. The Church, composed of [human beings], was not made by [human hands]. She is not an organisation. She is a living organism.[23]

This organism is the Mystical Body, the sacrament of Christ. De Lubac's ecclesiology, like his Christology, is an ecclesiology 'from above': its source is in God, not in man. This does not imply that the Church was pre-existent.

Highlighting the sacramental character of the Church does not blind de Lubac to the weaknesses of the Church as an institution. Acknowledging the Church as the Mystical Body of Christ, he goes to some lengths to stress the difference between Christ and the Church: unlike Christ, the humanity of the Church is sinful. He goes on to insist that the Church is more of a paradox than is Christ because she is at once 'a great mystery and wonderful sacrament' but also 'a stumbling block and a rock of scandal'.[24] We find a similar caution from Herbert Vorgrimler:

> It is part of the Church's sacramentality that the Church is
> not identical with the saving reality contained within it, that
> it can fulfil its task of service as sign and instrument only in
> an imperfect way, and that in doing so, it often obstructs its
> own action.[25]

The human weakness and sinfulness of the Church and her priests do
not invalidate the effects of the sacraments. This was the error of the
Donatist heresy that St Augustine challenged. The reason why this
is an error is because it is Christ who is the source of grace, not the
Church. Christ, though present in the Church, may not be identified
with it: 'Jesus Christ and the Church may never be identified with one
another.'[26]

CHRISTOLOGICAL UNDERSTANDING OF CHURCH
All too often we only hear of the human and fragile side of the Church,
but the Church is not simply the institution made up of human beings.
Just as there are two natures in Christ we can speak of two elements
in the Church: the human and the divine.[27] In the case of the Church
the human side can fail and be sinful. This is not so of course with the
humanity of Christ. The parallel between the two natures in Christ
and the two elements in the Church, human and divine, helps us to
distinguish between the failures of the Church on the one hand and
the divine side of the Church on the other. The Church is the Body of
Christ; it is a spiritual reality that will not be destroyed.

CONCLUSION
As noted in the introduction of this book, one of the main distinguishing
marks of Christianity is the concept of sacrament. The sacraments play
a vital role in our pastoral practice and are central to our ecclesiology
and Christology. Our understanding of grace is an integral part of
sacramentology. From both a pastoral and theological point of view we
are constantly challenged to understand and integrate sacramentality
into our Christian life. That challenge is all the more demanding and
urgent in the wake of the Covid-19 pandemic, when sacraments were
not available for long periods.

 What we have tried to achieve in this first chapter is to move away
from a mechanical view of sacraments as isolated events that make

God present. The way we have done this is by focusing on Christ as the sacrament of God and the Church as the sacrament of Christ. Every sacramental celebration is an act of the Church and an act of Christ.

Our next chapter will explore the history of the sacraments; their development in the early centuries of Christianity and, in the case of marriage, its recognition as a sacrament as late as the second millennium. This historical exploration will give rise to the question of the source of the sacraments: were they instituted by Christ or are they the creation of the Church?

Notes

1   Pope Paul VI, *Evangelii Nuntiandi*, 1975, 47.

2   Heinrich Denzinger, *Enchiridion Symbolorum: Compendium of Creeds, Definitions, and Declarations on Matters of Faith and Morals*, 43rd edn, ed. Peter Hünermann, Robert Fastiggi and Anne Englund Nash, San Francisco: Ignatius Press, 2012, 1310.

3   Pope Francis, *Desiderio Desideravi*, 2022, 44.

4   Herbert Vorgrimler, *Sacramental Theology*, Collegeville, trans. L.M. Maloney, Minnesota: Liturgical Press, 1992 [German orig.: *Sakramententheologie*, Düsseldorf: Patmos Verlag, 1987], p. 10.

5   Ibid., p. 16.

6   Jean-Philippe Revel, *Traité des sacrements: I. Baptême et sacramentalité*, Paris: Cerf, 2004, p. 24. Translation my own.

7   Pope St Leo the Great, 'Sermon 2 on the Ascension', *The Divine Office* II, London: Harper Collins, 1974, p. 642.

8   Pope Francis, *Desiderio Desideravi*, 9.

9   Karl Rahner, *Über die Sakramente der Kirche*, Freiburg: Herder Verlag, 1985 [French edition: *Les Sacraments de l'Eglise*, trans. Marc Debacker, Paris: Nouvelle cité, 1987, pp. 12–14].

10 Karl Rahner, 'The Theology of the Symbol' in *Theological Investigations*, Vol. 4, trans. Kevin Smyth, Baltimore: Helicon Press and London: Darton, Longman & Todd, 1966, pp. 221–52, at p. 241.

11 Vorgrimler, *Sacramental Theology*, p. 34.

12 Karl Rahner, *Foundations of the Christian Faith: An Introduction to the Idea of Christianity*, trans. William V. Dych, New York: Crossroad, 1978, 2000, p. 419.

13 Vatican II, *Dei Verbum*, 1965, 2.

14 Rahner, 'The Theology of the Symbol', p. 251.

15 Avery Dulles, *Models of Revelation*, Maryknoll, New York: Orbis Books, 1983, 1992, 2014, p. 158.

16 Vatican II, *Lumen Gentium*, 1964, 48. Emphasis added.

17 Pope John Paul II, *Ecclesia de Eucharistia*, 2003, 24, citing *Lumen Gentium*, 1.

18 St Cyprian, *Epist.* 69; 6; PL 3, 1142 B, quoted in *Lumen Gentium, 9*, note 1. We take account of the fact that, from the third century, the term 'sacramentum' was used in reference to the sacraments. Hence the reference by Cyprian to the Church as *sacramentum* is significant.

19 Henri de Lubac, *Catholicism: Christ and the Common Destiny of Man*, trans. L.C. Sheppard and E. Englund, San Francisco: Ignatius Press, 1988 [French orig.: *Catholicisme: les aspects sociaux du dogme*, Paris: Cerf, 1938, 2003], p. 76.

20 Ibid., p. 82.

21 Ibid., p. 87.

22 Henri de Lubac, *The Splendor of the Church*, trans. Michael Mason, San Francisco: Ignatius Press, 1986, 1989 [French orig.: *Méditation sur l'Église*, Paris: Editions Montaigne, 1953], p. 204.

23 Henri de Lubac, *The Motherhood of the Church*, San Francisco: Ignatius Press, 1982 [French orig.: *Les églises particulières dans l'Église universelle*, Paris: Aubier Montaigne, 1971], p. 15.

24 De Lubac, *The Splendor of the Church*, p. 50. See Isaiah 8:14; Romans 9:33; 1 Peter 2:8.

25 Vorgrimler, *Sacramental Theology*, p. 37.

26 Ibid., p. 22.

27 Among those who argued for a parallel between the two natures in Christ and the twofold element in the Church is Yves Congar. See 'Dogme christologique et ecclésiologie. Vérité et limites d'un parallèle', in *Das Konzil von Chalkedon. Geschichte und Gegenwart*, Vol. 3, Würzburg: Echter Verlag, 1954, pp. 239–68.

CHAPTER TWO

HOW DID THE SACRAMENTS DEVELOP?

INTRODUCTION

The title of this chapter implies that the sacraments were not handed on by Christ as ready-made rites that have retained their every detail since New Testament times. To express it rather graphically, Jesus did not make the first confession box in his workshop in Nazareth! We will see that there was a development that had its roots in the action and preaching of Christ. Some sacraments can more readily be identified in scripture, but the term 'sacrament' is not found in scripture at all. We will trace the origins of the term and then proceed to examine how the Church eventually decided on seven sacraments: baptism, confirmation, Eucharist, penance, anointing of the sick, holy orders and matrimony. Of course, it is important to keep in mind that the different ecclesial communions that have their origin in the Reformation do not accept all seven sacraments. They usually propose baptism and Eucharist as the only sacraments. But it is not just the Reformers who debated the identity of the sacraments. The first millennium of the Church is marked by debate and disagreement as to what constitutes a sacrament. The early centuries of the second millennium record prolonged debates on the issue before reaching agreement in the fifteenth century.

The question arises as to the origin of the term 'sacrament', a question that is particularly pertinent since the term is not found in scripture. So, we need to elaborate our question as we set out to understand the Christian sacraments. This setting out of the question is known as the 'problematic'. The problematic in relation to the sacraments may be set out as follows.

SACRAMENTS NOT GIVEN IN DEFINITIVE FORM

The term *sacramentum* was introduced into the Latin language of the Church at the beginning of the third century. So we need to research its origins, not only as a term but in respect to the reality it claimed to express. The core element in our quest is the scriptural basis for sacraments, especially in our ecumenical dialogue. If the sacraments cannot be traced back to Christ, can we presume that they are simply man-made? Born-again Christians would dismiss the idea of sacraments as a buffer set up by the Church between the individual and Christ. So our understanding of sacraments is not a cosy academic question. It is vital for our confidence in our Christian tradition. I use the term 'Christian' and not 'Catholic' advisedly because the Protestant communions have sacraments as well, though usually fewer in number than do Catholics.

Closely related to the question of origins is the following critical issue. Individual sacraments are performed using certain material objects, together with a formula of words, and are usually celebrated by an ordained priest or deacon. The sacraments are said to bring about the reality they signify. Does this mean that they can be performed somehow independently of God? What is the relationship between the celebration of a sacrament and the action of God in the world?

If we bring the two questions together we may express our problematic like this: we are concerned about the link between Christ and the sacraments in their origin and we are equally keen to show that God is part of every sacrament; indeed that there can be no sacrament without his presence. We will further refine these questions in the course of this chapter.

One possible starting point on our journey is scripture. If we start there, however, we will see that most of the questions that arise later in the history of the sacraments were not issues for the writers of the New Testament. For this reason, we will take another point of departure, one that will lead back to scripture. We will trace the historical development of the sacraments from the early centuries of the Church until the Middle Ages when they are firmly established as seven in number and when the issues we have raised are settled.

In the first millennium the number of sacraments varied between two and twelve. Those who claimed there were two sacraments were pointing to baptism and the Eucharist, both of which are clearly scriptural in origin. The names associated with this view are Fulbert of Chartres (*c*.952–1028) and Bruno of Würzburg (*c*.1005–45). At the other end of the scale we find St Bernard of Clairvaux OCist (1090–1153) and St Peter Damian OSB (1007–72). For Bernard, a sacrament was a sacred sign that communicated grace. He claimed there were ten such sacred signs and included in his list the washing of the feet and the investiture of bishops, canons and abbots. Peter Damian proposed a total of twelve sacraments, including in his list the consecration of a king, the dedication of a church and the consecration of virgins. Peter Lombard (*c*.1100–60), on the other hand, suggested that there were seven sacraments. The sacramentaries of this period describe Lent as the 'venerable sacrament'. Sometimes the term sacrament was applied to the entire activity of the Spirit in relation to the soul.

For the first two centuries the word used for the reality that was later to be called a sacrament was the Greek term *musterion* (mystery). This term seemed appropriate because it was used in the Greek translation of the Old Testament, i.e., the Septuagint.[1] *Musterion* means secret. Interestingly, the Gaelic translation of 'mystery' in this sense is *rundiamhar Dé*, which literally means 'secret of God'. But the word mystery gave rise to problems: it was used in the pagan cultures of the time and so it was considered ambiguous. In Greek philosophy, for example, tangible things were regarded as symbols of heavenly reality and the initiated learned secret teachings (mysteries) that brought them wisdom. The use of the term 'mystery' was particularly prevalent in Gnosticism.[2] This led to an unease about its use for Christian rites. To this day, however, the Eastern Orthodox Church employs the term *musterion* for the rites called sacraments in the West.

A new term was provided by Tertullian (*c*.160–*c*.225), who suggested the legal word *sacramentum*, from the verb *sacrare*, meaning to swear an oath. On entering the military a young man would swear an oath, and at the time this was seen as having a religious significance. Tertullian used the term to express entry to the Church, i.e. baptism, which became known as a *sacramentum*. Gradually it spread to the other mysteries (sacraments) and was taken up by subsequent theologians or Fathers of the Church, especially St Cyprian and St Hilary of Poitiers (*c*.315–*c*.367). St Hilary gave the term *sacramentum* its full meaning, as an effective producer of grace.[3]

For St Augustine, a *sacramentum* was a visible sign to which corresponded an invisible part, effecting a spiritual reality. Augustine introduced the term *res* (reality) in connection with *sacramentum* to distinguish between the sacrament of Christ's body (the Eucharist) and the reality or effect of the sacrament when received. Augustine used the term *res* to express the ultimate effect of the Eucharist, that is, the grace of union with Christ and the union of Christians in the Body of Christ (the Church). In simple terms, the *sacramentum* is what is seen on the altar, while the *res* is the reality brought about among the participants. In the eleventh century this notion will be expanded when theologians debate questions of eucharistic presence. For Augustine, sacraments are effective because Christ and the Holy Spirit act through them. He regards the role of the ordained minister as essential but subordinate. According to the Doctor of Grace, baptism and certain other sacraments have permanent effects: they place a seal on the soul of the recipient that will never be erased. Later theology will call this seal the sacramental 'character'. The term 'seal' can be misleading because it implies something physical, whereas 'character' is more judicious. It means that the baptised person has a new and lasting relationship with Christ and the Church.

St Thomas Aquinas offers a well-rounded understanding of 'character', on which Liam Walsh OP comments as follows:

> One of the most creative parts of Thomas' theology of sacraments is what he has to say about character (q. 63). … Thomas is able to develop Augustine's thinking about the seal without the pressure of any polemic and to use it to clarify important ecclesiological and Christological features of the rites called sacraments.[4]

Furthermore, Walsh makes more explicit the Christological and ecclesial dimensions of sacraments:

The accent is less on how it marks the soul than on how it gives an ecclesiological and Christological qualification to human action, which allows a person to make ritual signs that are, and are recognised to be, acts of the Church and of Christ, and therefore grace-bearing.[5]

In addition to baptism, the sacraments of confirmation and holy orders (priesthood) confer a permanent character. This means that from the reception of each of these sacraments a person has a new relationship with Christ and his Church. We will see what this involves in detail in later chapters, but a brief description is warranted here. Baptism welcomes one into the Body of Christ and this is a permanent state. In confirmation a person becomes a witness to Christ and his Church or, as Pope Francis opines, we become missionary disciples. The sacrament of orders consecrates and empowers the candidate to represent Christ, the head of the Church, especially in the celebration of the sacraments.

INSTITUTION BY CHRIST

The *Catechism of the Catholic Church* (*CCC*), following the teaching of the Council of Trent (1545–63), states: "Adhering to the teaching of the Holy Scriptures, to the apostolic traditions, and to the consensus … of the Fathers", we profess that "the sacraments of the new law were … all instituted by Jesus Christ our Lord'" (*CCC*, 1114).[6]

Hugh of St Victor (*c.*1096–1141) made a major contribution to the development of our understanding of sacraments, highlighting three characteristics, including institution by Christ:

1. The aptitude of the material element to represent, through natural likeness, what it signified (*ex similitudine repraesentans*). This is easily appreciated in terms of baptism and the Eucharist, as we will see later, though more difficult to establish in some of the other sacraments, like penance.
2. Reference to the institution of the sacrament by Christ, who established the link between the material element and grace (*ex institutione significans*). Again, this is clearly evident in baptism and the Eucharist but less so in relation to the other sacraments, especially marriage.

3. The work of sanctification (*ex sanctificatione continens*).
    Sacraments sanctify the participants.

With Hugh of St Victor the institution of the sacrament by Christ became the distinguishing element, without which one couldn't speak of sacraments. The above quote from the *Catechism of the Catholic Church* emphasises the same point. However, a critical question arises at this point: what does institution by Christ mean? We shall see in subsequent chapters how each of the sacraments developed over the centuries. Here we will give an outline of what institution means in terms of baptism and the Eucharist. We will also look at the possibility for seeing a basis in scripture for the sacraments of penance and anointing.

Baptism and Eucharist are easily evidenced as being instituted explicitly by Christ. We find in Matthew's gospel that Jesus commissions his apostles to baptise:

> Now the eleven disciples went to Galilee, to the mountain to which Jesus had directed them. When they saw him, they worshipped him; but some doubted. And Jesus came and said to them, 'All authority in heaven and on earth has been given to me. Go therefore and make disciples of all nations, baptising them in the name of the Father and of the Son and of the Holy Spirit, and teaching them to obey everything that I have commanded you. And remember, I am with you always, to the end of the age.' (Mt 28:16-20)

The Great Commission, as this passage is known, makes clear that the Church has been given the mission to baptise. We will see in our chapter on baptism that the details of how this sacrament would be celebrated were yet to be discovered.

The Eucharist is likewise a sacrament explicitly gifted by Christ, though of course neither baptism nor the Eucharist is called a sacrament by Jesus. There are four occasions in the New Testament that record the institution of the Eucharist: 1 Corinthians 11:23-6, Luke 22:19-20, Mark 14:22-4 and Matthew 26:26-8. These are known as the institution narratives. Two of these make explicit that Jesus intends his apostles to do what Jesus has done at the Last Supper: 'Do this in remembrance of me' (1 Corinthians and Luke).

However, the other sacraments are more challenging in our quest for a scriptural basis. The ministry of forgiveness and healing is a strong indicator that the Church will continue that ministry. We remember the words of Jesus to the apostles following the resurrection: 'Receive the Holy Spirit. If you forgive the sins of any, they are forgiven them; if you retain the sins of any, they are retained' (Jn 20:22-3). The sacrament of penance, as we know it today, went through many developments before it reached its present liturgical practice. We will see this in detail in chapter 5.

In relation to the sacrament of the sick we can point to the Letter of St James:

> Are any among you sick? They should call for the elders of the church and have them pray over them, anointing them with oil in the name of the Lord. The prayer of faith will save the sick, and the Lord will raise them up; and anyone who has committed sins will be forgiven. (Jas 5:14-15)

James is obviously referring to a practice rather than proposing something novel. So these are strong indications that the ministry of forgiveness and healing continued after Jesus, though they weren't called sacraments as we call them now.

Though Jesus Christ did not give us a template for these sacraments, this does not mean that he did not institute them: he did so by his life, message and ministry. Liam Walsh captures the subtlety of the relationship between the sacraments and their institution by Christ in this remark:

> Christ is seen to institute a sacrament as much by what he was and did, and by the imagery and historical tradition in which his life was expressed, as by commands he gave to perform certain rites.[7]

In later chapters we will see that the institution of the episcopate and priesthood is far more gradual than is the case with baptism and the Eucharist. Marriage in particular has an exceptionally long genesis.

DIFFICULTIES WITH THE TERM 'SYMBOL'

Continuing through the history of sacraments leads us to a controversy in the Middle Ages that resulted in further clarification of the meaning of sacraments. It centred on Berengar of Tours (*c.*1010–88). Berengar compared the water of baptism to the bread and wine of the Eucharist and claimed that just as water symbolises the cleansing graces of Christ, so the bread and wine merely symbolise the body and blood of Christ. He denied that Christ's true body was present in the sacrament. He held that there were two elements to a sacrament: the external sign or symbol (*sacramentum*) and the ultimate effect, the grace of spiritual nourishment and charity (*res*).

In order to preserve the symbolism of the Eucharist and to safeguard the reality of Christ's presence in the Eucharist, eleventh-century theologians, such as Archbishop of Canterbury Lanfranc OSB (*c.*1005–1089), searched for a third element to describe the sacramental action to safeguard the fact that the consecrated bread and wine are changed into the body and blood of Christ and as such are totally different from the water of baptism. A definitive formulation was established by Hugh of St Victor and Peter Lombard in the twelfth century and endorsed by Pope Innocent III (1160/1–1216) at the beginning of the thirteenth century. Alongside the already established dimensions of the nature of sacraments – *sacramentum tantum* (the sacramental rite) and *res tantum* (the grace/fruit or the sacrament) – they added *sacramentum et res* (the sacrament and the reality).

Vorgrimler explains why the three dimensions need to be articulated in relation to sacraments:

> A threefold distinction was important: the external sign, consisting of matter and form, is only a sign and is not yet its content. It is called *sacramentum* or external sacrament. The content, the ultimate effect of the sacrament, that is, the grace of God, is not, for its own part, a sign. It is called the *res sacramenti* (the effect of the sacrament). Finally, there is a middle term between the two: it is brought into the visible realm by the first, external sign, and it immediately produces the second, grace. This middle is called *res et sacramentum* (the reality and the sign together), or internal sacrament.[8]

The difficulties created by Berengar of Tours led to an expansion of Augustine's teaching on sacraments. It would no longer suffice to think in terms of the *sacramentum* and the effects of the *sacramentum* in those who participated. It became essential also to emphasise the reality of Christ's presence in the Eucharist. The term 'transubstantiation' had yet to be applied to the Eucharist.

CAUSALITY

The second aspect of our problematic concerning the relationship between the material elements of a sacrament and the action of God is treated by St Thomas Aquinas. He rethought theological questions using the philosophy of Aristotle, with which he became familiar through the Latin translations of the Greek philosopher's work by the Muslim scholar Averroes (1126–98). For Aquinas, the sacraments effect what they signify (*efficiunt quod figurant*).[9] Peter Lombard had also proposed this definition of sacraments. It is an understanding of sacraments that we find in the *Catechism of the Catholic Church*:

> The sacraments are perceptible signs (words and actions) accessible to our human nature. By the action of Christ and the power of the Holy Spirit they make present efficaciously the grace that they signify. (*CCC*, 1084)

When Aquinas describes how sacraments as signs cause grace he distinguishes between two kinds of efficient causes: principal and instrumental. Since only God can produce the effect of sanctification, he alone can be called the principal cause. Thus, sacraments are instrumental causes; they work only by virtue of the impetus given them by the principal cause, God.[10] His distinction between instrumental causality, which includes the material used (the sign), and the principal cause, who is God, enabled him to conceptualise what had for so long remained elusive. He illustrated the distinction between instrumental and principal causality using the very earthy image of the workman and the hatchet. The hatchet is the tool used to cut the timber that will eventually become a bed. The hatchet alone would not bring about the piece of furniture; there needs to be a principal cause who is the workman. The bed doesn't resemble the hatchet but the project contained in the mind of the workman. Using this analogy, Aquinas made clear that God is always the source of the sanctification (the principal cause), while the sacramental rite is the instrumental cause. Aquinas' definition of causality is normative in our understanding of sacraments. For this reason, some attempts to rethink the sacraments in terms of symbol, thereby challenging the idea of causality, have run into difficulty.[11] From our first chapter we made clear that it is possible to think of sacraments in symbolic terms using the understanding of symbol we find in modern theologians like Karl Rahner.

In this connection the distinction between *ex opere operato* ('by the work done') and *ex opere operantis* ('by the work of the doer') is important. *Ex opere operato* means that sacraments are effective by means of the sacramental rite itself, not because of the worthiness of the minister or participant. *Ex opere operantis* means that the effectiveness of sacraments depends on the moral rectitude of the minister or participant. The efficaciousness of Christian sacraments does not depend on the worthiness of the minister. Vorgrimler comments:

> 'By the power of the completed ritual' (*ex opere operato*) thus means that the sacrament derives its validity and effectiveness from the power of God. Human religious subjectivity, human faith, human readiness to accept pardon and salvation from God are *not* the *cause* of the sacrament's effective power; they are the *condition*, brought about by the Spirit of God, for the effective application of the grace of God that is offered in the sacrament.[12]

And again:

> Since Jesus Christ is the one who is really acting in the sacraments, their inner, sacred reality and effect cannot be damaged by unworthy ministers.[13]

SEVEN SACRAMENTS

The number of sacraments was only formally defined at the Council of Florence with the bull *Exultate Deo*, promulgated on 22 November 1439.[14] It was the (unknown) author of the *Summa Sententiarum* who had designated the number seven, but with Peter Lombard it became part of the systematic teaching of theology.

Notes

1   The Septuagint is the translation of the Old Testament from the original Hebrew into Greek. It dates from the third century BCE. The name is derived from the Latin word for 'seventy', *septuaginta*, the belief being that seventy scholars worked on this translation in Alexandria.

2   The name 'gnostic' derives from the Greek word *gnosis*, meaning knowledge. Gnosticism means that salvation is achieved through knowledge. It was a complex religious movement contemporaneous to early Christianity.

3   *Dictionnaire de Théologie Catholique*, Paris: Librairie Letouzey et Ané, 1939, Vol. 14.1, col. 493.

4   Liam G. Walsh OP, *Sacraments of Initiation: A Theology of Life, Word, and Rite*, Chicago: Liturgy Training Publications, 2011, p. 30.

5   Ibid., p. 79.

6   See also, Heinrich Denzinger, *Enchiridion Symbolorum: Compendium of Creeds, Definitions, and Declarations on Matters of Faith and Morals*, 43rd edn, ed. Peter Hünermann, Robert Fastiggi and Anne Englund Nash, San Francisco: Ignatius Press, 2012, 1600–1.

7   Walsh, *Sacraments of Initiation*, p. 76.

8   Herbert Vorgrimler, *Sacramental Theology*, Collegeville, trans. L.M. Maloney, Minnesota: Liturgical Press, 1992 [German orig.: *Sakramententheologie*, Düsseldorf: Patmos Verlag, 1987], p. 54.

9   St Thomas Aquinas, *Summa Theologiae*, IIIa, q. 62, a. 1, ad primum.

10 See Aquinas, *Summa Theologiae*, IIIa, q. 62, a. 1 Respondeo.

11 See, for example, Louis-Marie Chauvet, *Symbole et sacrement: Une relecture sacramentelle de l'existence chrétienne*, Paris: Cerf, 1987, pp. 47–8. See art. 'Sacrements', in *Dictionnaire encyclopédique du Moyen Âge*, tome II, Vauchez, André (dir.), Paris: Cerf, 1997, pp. 1355–57.

12 Vorgrimler, *Sacramental Theology*, p. 87.

13 Ibid., p. 50.

14 Denzinger, *Enchiridion Symbolorum*, 1310.

CHAPTER THREE

SACRAMENTS OF CHRISTIAN INITIATION I: BAPTISM AND CONFIRMATION

INTRODUCTION

Full Christian initiation involves baptism, confirmation and Eucharist, but the first of all the sacraments is always baptism. Without this, the other sacraments cannot be received. While infant baptism is the usual pastoral praxis, our understanding of baptism can be accessed more accurately by thinking in terms of adult baptism, i.e. an adult coming to an informed decision to want to be a Christian and requesting the sacraments in faith. This is a request that is made to the Church. It is immediately obvious then that a theology of Christian initiation is inseparably linked to a theology of the Church. For our purposes here we will come to a better understanding of the sacraments of initiation if we approach them from the perspective of adults rather than infants.

SACRAMENTS IN A SYNODAL CHURCH

RCIA PROGRAMME

Many parishes now have a Rite of Christian Initiation of Adults (RCIA) programme to guide and prepare adults as they enter the Catholic faith. This rite is based on the catechumenal process that was employed in the Church from the second to the fifth centuries in the East and the West, and was revived following the Second Vatican Council. The catechumenate proceeds in four stages: the pre-catechumenate of initial evangelisation; the catechumenate in which there is continued evangelisation and catechesis; the period of immediate preparation for the sacraments of initiation; and the post-initiation catechesis and more active participation in the life of the Church.

The current pastoral practice is that a group of lay people are trained to accompany those who have asked for baptism; the latter are called 'catechumens'. The preparation takes two to three years. We read in the Introduction to the *Rite of Christian Initiation of Adults*:

> The initiation of catechumens is a gradual process that takes place within the community of the faithful. By joining the catechumens in reflecting on the value of the paschal mystery and by renewing their own conversion, the faithful provide an example that will help the catechumens to obey the Holy Spirit more generously.[1]

This introduction emphasises a number of important points that deserve some comment: the Church, the paschal mystery, conversion, Christian witness and obedience to the Holy Spirit.

The preparation for baptism takes place within the Church, as represented by the local parish (or group of parishes). After an initial pre-catechumenate period of evangelisation, one is admitted as a candidate for baptism. This can be done publicly at Sunday Mass when the candidate is introduced to the congregation. The candidate may wish to speak and say why they are taking this step. This can be a powerful witness in itself, even before they begin the formal preparation for baptism. It is challenging to hear someone tell a congregation, 'I want to become a Catholic because …'. Of course, the relationship is reciprocal: the Church community witnesses to the prospective new Christian and undertakes to give their support. There is something quite moving about the relationship between the catechumens and the established Church. The new enliven the old; the old impart the gift of their lived Christian lives. One challenges and inspires the other.

At the end of the catechumenate period, once the RCIA team is satisfied that the catechumen is ready, the initiation takes place, preferably at the Easter Vigil on Holy Saturday night. It is now normal practice that the three sacraments of initiation are administered on that occasion: baptism, confirmation and Eucharist. The parish priest is delegated by the bishop to impart the sacrament of confirmation, a sacrament normally reserved to the bishop. A powerfully symbolic part of that ceremony is the exchange of the purple scarf that was worn throughout Lent for a white scarf symbolising the new life of the Christian. In the Paris archdiocese, where a large number of adult baptisms take place at the Easter Vigil throughout the city, it is impressive to see young adults received into the Church. They will be familiar to parishioners throughout Lent with their distinctive purple scarves. After the Vigil the distinctive white scarf is a notable witness to the new life of Easter.

SACRAMENTS AND THE PASCHAL MYSTERY

It is not without significance that the ideal time for Christian initiation is Easter. This is because the Church celebrates the death and resurrection of Christ at this time. We call this the 'paschal mystery'. It is from Christ's death and resurrection that the new life flows to the baptised. Indeed, it is the paschal mystery that is the source of all the sacraments. Baptism is the descent into the death of Christ, symbolised by immersion in water, and it is at one and the same time a rising to the life of the resurrected Christ. It involves the forgiveness of sins and the gift of grace. Part of the baptismal preparation, therefore, involves a process of conversion that is helped by the RCIA programme and the witness of the Christian community. Throughout, the catechumen is guided by the Holy Spirit to make this conversion, which involves renouncing sin and confessing Jesus as Lord: '… no-one can say "Jesus is Lord" except by the Holy Spirit' (1 Cor 12:3). For Paul, this marks a turning-point in our lives. In Romans 8:10-11 we learn that this conversion is due to the work of the Holy Spirit within us. In this new form of life, the Spirit makes us sons and daughters of God. We can speak to God in that familiar way that Jesus himself used, calling him 'Abba, Father' (Mk 14:36). We now have access to God not, as formerly, to the fearsome Almighty One, but as to a loving Father. In this way the Holy Spirit leads us into a new life of faith and prayer:

> But if Christ is in you, though the body is dead because of sin, the Spirit is life because of righteousness. If the Spirit of him who raised Jesus from the dead dwells in you, he who raised Christ from the dead will give life to your mortal bodies also through his Spirit that dwells in you. (Rm 8:10-11)

The Spirit enlivens us. This is another way of speaking of the grace of the sacrament. It is especially in the Letter to the Romans that we find a rich theology of baptism, where Paul makes clear the connection between the paschal mystery and baptism:

> Do you not know that all of us who have been baptised into Christ Jesus were baptised into his death? Therefore we have been buried with him by baptism into death, so that, just as Christ was raised from the dead by the glory of the Father, so we too might walk in newness of life. For if we have been united with him in a death like his, we will certainly be united with him in a resurrection like his. We know that our old self was crucified with him so that the body of sin might be destroyed, and we might no longer be enslaved to sin. For whoever has died is freed from sin. But if we have died with Christ, we believe that we will also live with him. (Rm 6:3-8)

St Paul gives us a profound and mysterious notion of the grace of baptism. For the apostle, the death and resurrection of Christ form the watershed from which all the graces of salvation come to us (Rm 4:25). Our baptism is our first immersion in that mystery of Christ's death and resurrection. As Paul understands it, we share in Christ's death by dying to our old selves, and we are said to rise with him by coming to share in the graces of his risen life. There is further evidence of this understanding of baptism in the Pauline corpus; it occurs in Colossians: 'When you were buried with him in baptism, you were also raised with him through faith in the power of God, who raised him from the dead' (Col 2:12). Full immersion in water is the symbol of entering into the death of Christ and rising with him. The term baptism is derived from the Greek *baptizein,* meaning to immerse, to plunge.

GRACE

As we are using the term 'grace' so frequently, a brief exposition is required. Grace (*charis, gratia*) has its theological origin in the New Testament, though it existed in the Septuagint. It occurs some one hundred times in the Pauline and Deutero-Pauline writings, and perhaps fifty times in the rest of the New Testament, where its use suggests 'kindness', 'favour' and the benevolence of God.[2] In addition to Paul's use of this term in his greetings, he also employs it to refer to his apostolic calling, for example 'by the grace God gave me' (1 Cor 3:10), meaning his vocation.[3] In Romans, Paul attributes justification to grace: ' They [Jew and pagan] are now justified by his grace as a gift, through the redemption that is in Christ Jesus' (Rm 3:24). Paul uses it especially in his greetings and valedictions, for example: 'The grace of our Lord Jesus Christ, the love of God and the fellowship of the Holy Spirit be with you all'(2 Cor 13:13).

But Paul did not use the word we translate as 'grace' as a sharply defined concept with a concern for theological consistency. Cornelius Ernst OP (1924–77) comments:

> We might say that he used it poetically, meaning that under the pressure of powerful enthusiastic feeling the word excited associations and even perhaps created them when Paul set about preaching the gospel of God's transcendent generosity to man in Jesus Christ.[4]

In summary, grace is a term used of a wide range of experiences, but it always implies the activity of the Holy Spirit in us.

INCORPORATION INTO THE CHURCH

Baptism is not just entrance into the paschal mystery of dying and rising with Christ; it is also a baptism into the body of Christ, the Church:

> For just as the body is one and has many members, and all the members of the body, though many, are one body, so it is with Christ. For in the one Spirit we were all baptised

into one body – Jews or Greeks, slaves or free – and we were all made to drink of one Spirit. Indeed, the body does not consist of one member but of many. (1 Cor 12:12-14)

Becoming a Christian is not an isolated individualistic act; it involves becoming part of a community. The community has a responsibility to continue to support, witness to and challenge the new Christian. For example, the moral life is a consequence and a living out of the baptismal participation in the paschal mystery. The ongoing formation of those newly initiated into the Church is an important responsibility for the RCIA team, for the parish and for the diocese. It would be disillusioning for someone to find the great flourish at their baptism petered out once they were initiated.

THE ORIGINS OF BAPTISM

The practice of baptism goes back to the very origins of the Christian Church. First there was the ministry of John the Baptist. The ritual washing at that stage was only a prefiguring of the Christian sacrament. John's ritual was all about forgiveness of sin in order to escape the wrath of God at the end of the world, which many people of the time thought was imminent. Jesus was baptised by John to identify with sinful humanity, though he was without sin himself. As a result, from then on, the ritual began to have a new meaning. The heavens were opened; the Father spoke; the Holy Spirit descended (Mk 1:9-11). The ritual was radically changed: the presence of the Father, the Son and the Holy Spirit make it a Trinitarian experience.

The basic reality of baptism lies in the fact that people are not born Christians; they have to become Christians. Baptism is the beginning of that process. It is not a once-off, an end in itself; it is the gateway to Christianity and the door of the Church.

INFANT BAPTISM

When baptism is spoken of in the early Church, they usually have adult baptism in mind. Infant baptism should be seen as an exceptional instance of the sacrament, since the child is incapable of that explicit act of committed faith that the sacraments normally require. However, the practice of infant baptism is witnessed to explicitly from the second century on. It was probably already practised in the apostolic Church and is most likely implicit in statements about whole households being baptised by the apostles (see, for example, Acts 16:15, 16:33, 18:8 and 1 Cor 1:16). The second- to third-century theologian Hippolytus of Rome (*c*.170–*c*.235) mentions the initiation of children. The reason for the baptism of children in this period is likely to have been family solidarity rather than concerns about original sin, as was the case later.[5] St Augustine drew attention to the practice of infant baptism as a theological argument to prove original sin was antecedent to any personal sin.

The question of infant baptism was hotly debated in the sixteenth century. The Reformers were concerned because they regarded faith as an essential pre-requisite to sacramental participation. Martin Luther (1483–1546) oscillated in regard to infant baptism and the possible reasons for it. He considered children as being most suitable for baptism because they offered less resistance to God's grace than did adults. Then he evoked Christ welcoming and blessing children and promising them the kingdom. In baptism the children meet the same Christ. Ultimately, for Luther, God's love is sufficient to give theological justification to infant baptism. Similarly, John Calvin (1509–64) argued for infant baptism because the Holy Spirit nurtures the beginnings of faith and repentance in infants. Furthermore, infants are part of the covenant and the community. Finally, the Council of Trent strongly supported the practice of infant baptism and counted baptised infants as part of the faithful.

The debate on infant baptism came to a head again in the twentieth century. A strong opponent was the Swiss Reformed theologian Karl Barth (1886–1968), who regarded it as unthinkable that baptism was possible apart from a willing and ready recipient. He strongly objected to the Roman Catholic sacramental practice of an objective celebration of baptism. However, he was vehemently opposed by two significant theologians: Oscar Cullmann (1902–99), a Lutheran, and Heinrich Schlier (1900–78), an evangelical theologian who converted to Catholicism in 1953. Cullmann, a New Testament scholar, argued that the effects of baptism are independent of faith and, thereby, justified infant baptism. Schlier argued, on the basis of sacraments being effective *ex opere operato*, that infant baptism is valid. He did, however, emphasise that adult baptism should be accompanied by faith. In 1982 the 'Lima Document' of the World Council of Churches acknowledged the two forms of the sacrament: adult believer's baptism and infant baptism. In both cases baptism is a work of God in Christ.[6]

From a Roman Catholic point of view the practice of infant baptism fits in with our teaching on grace in so far as grace is essentially prior to any human act. Nor does the practice of infant baptism violate any human law or individual freedom. The key thing is that the reality into which baptism incorporates the infant is something beneficial and indeed wonderful: from now on they are a son or daughter of God. Just as we have no difficulty in incorporating babies into all kinds of human structures once they are beneficial, for instance the education system, the community, the state, so too we incorporate them into God's family, the Church. From the moment of baptism, the infant belongs to God in a new way, and is placed into a whole new stream of God's providence and loving care as his very own son or daughter.

EFFECTS OF CHURCH EXPANSION ON BAPTISMAL THEOLOGY AND PRACTICE

By the fourth century the number of baptisms of both adults and infants grew to such an extent that they could not be confined to Easter and Pentecost. In addition, the bishop could not be present at these ceremonies as heretofore. The catechumenate programme was not practised with the same thoroughness as had been the case previously. In 416 the bishop was designated as the ordinary minister of the final anointing (in the Gallican rites the priest was the ordinary minister of this anointing until the Middle Ages). Eventually this final part of the rite, associated with the gift of the Holy Spirit, became separated from the baptismal rite itself and may be at the origin of the sacrament of confirmation. In any case, we can be sure that from the fourth century initiation developed into two sacraments, baptism and confirmation, the first performed by the priest or deacon, the second reserved to the bishop.

Regis Duffy OFM (1934–2006) gives a summary of the changes that took place following the wide expansion of the Church:

> First, the ecclesial dimension of the sacrament had become mute, if not lost. Baptism was received for the forgiveness of sin, but the importance of incorporation into the body of Christ was gradually eclipsed. As this one-dimensional theology became predominant, the teaching of Augustine on 'character' in initiation became distorted and the role of the Holy Spirit in the whole process of conversion and initiation was obscured.[7]

When the ecclesial dimension of the sacraments is lost, they become individualistic. The reference to the forgiveness of sin in baptism is worthy of comment. Unlike our current practice, forgiveness was a once-off event. There was no sacrament of reconciliation as we know it. For this reason, people postponed baptism for as long as possible to ensure that they were forgiven before death. This reasoning distorted greatly the intention of Christian initiation. It was a diminishment of the sacrament of baptism to see it in terms of forgiveness of sins alone; the community dimension and the sense of becoming part of the body of Christ were ignored. 'Character' came to be regarded as an interior quality and its original external quality of ecclesial and liturgical participation was lost. Similarly, the role of the Holy Spirit in the Christian life, especially in relation to conversion, was obscured. Nowadays, 'character' is understood in its original pristine sense with emphasis on the identification of the new Christian as linked to Christ, together with the ecclesial context of the sacraments linked to character.

The Second Vatican Council set out clearly both a theological understanding of baptism and a clear outline of the process of the catechumenate. Initiation is, first of all, entrance into the paschal mystery: 'In this sacred rite fellowship in Christ's death and resurrection is symbolised and is brought about.'[8] It is incorporation into a priestly and liturgical community: 'Incorporated into the Church by baptism, the faithful are appointed by their baptismal character to Christian religious worship.'[9] Further, 'In that Body all the faithful are made a holy and kingly priesthood; they offer spiritual sacrifices to God through Jesus Christ'.[10] From an ecumenical perspective the Council has an important message, namely that Christian initiation creates a bond of unity and a source of potentially full unity among the divided Christian communities: 'Baptism constitutes the sacramental bond of unity existing among all who through it are reborn. Baptism is ordained … toward a complete integration into Eucharistic communion.'[11] St Thomas Aquinas highlights the fact that baptism leads to Eucharist: 'Baptism is the beginning of the spiritual life and the door to the sacraments; whereas the Eucharist is, as it were, the summit of the spiritual life, and the goal of all the sacraments.'[12]

We can establish four principles in relation to the sacraments of initiation, and in particular baptism. First, that while infant baptism is common pastoral praxis, the theological norm remains the person capable of asking for these sacraments in faith. Second, that baptism, confirmation and Eucharist are united as initiating sacraments. Third, that the ecclesial community is central to the whole process of initiation. And finally, an important one to remember, that conversion is a gradual process.[13]

FROM ONE TO TWO RITES: BAPTISM AND CONFIRMATION

Confirmation has been described as a sacrament in search of a theology. This implies that we have a rite in the Church and there is lack of clarity as to its meaning. I disagree. I do so because there is strong evidence in the Acts of the Apostles to suggest a distinction between baptism and a rite that imparts the Holy Spirit. Again, it is important to remember that there is no explicit mention of sacraments in the scriptures. We will examine the relevant texts presently. First of all, I would like to focus on the promise of the Holy Spirit by Jesus at the Last Supper. There are five instances of this promise recorded in the Gospel of St John:

> John 14:16-17: 'And I will ask the Father, and he will give you another Advocate, to be with you for ever. This is the Spirit of truth, whom the world cannot receive, because it neither sees him nor knows him. You know him, because he abides with you, and he will be in you.'

> John 14:26: 'But the Advocate, the Holy Spirit, whom the Father will send in my name, will teach you everything, and remind you of all that I have said to you.'

> John 15:26: 'When the Advocate comes, whom I will send to you from the Father, the Spirit of truth who comes from the Father, he will testify on my behalf.'

> John 16:7: 'It is to your advantage that I go away, for if I do not go away, the Advocate will not come to you; but if I go, I will send him to you.'

> John 16:13: 'When the Spirit of truth comes, he will guide you into all the truth; for he will not speak on his own, but will speak whatever he hears, and he will declare to you the things that are to come.'

Obviously, Jesus considered as pivotal what would happen to his followers after the resurrection and ascension. He himself would no longer be a visible, physical presence to them. He promises to remain with them through the gift of the Holy Spirit, a gift that will come from the Father and the Son (*filioque*) and radically transform their lives. At the time of Jesus' death and resurrection his apostles had participated in the Eucharist (the first) and had all the graces that we now speak of in terms of baptism. They were not bereft of the Spirit at that point, but there was a powerful manifestation that was still awaited, namely Pentecost. While the apostles achieved certainty as to who Jesus was through their experience of his resurrection, they still remained frightened of the Jews and locked themselves away from human society. Neither did they fully understand the mission of Jesus and their part in it. They expected that he would 'restore the kingdom to Israel' (Acts 1:6). Jesus responds: 'You will receive power [*dunamin*] when the Holy Spirit has come upon you; and you will be my witnesses in Jerusalem, in all Judea and Samaria, and to the ends of the earth' (Acts 1:8). The key term in Jesus' promise here is *dunamis*, the power that will transform these frightened men into fearless apostles, to the extent of giving their lives for Christ. This is no inflated human courage; it is a divine ability to face opposition and challenge, irrespective of the cost to them personally. This power is imparted to them when the Holy Spirit comes upon them at Pentecost (Acts 2). Confirmation is our Pentecost.

'BE SEALED WITH THE GIFT OF THE HOLY SPIRIT'

Gifted with the Holy Spirit and now capable of understanding Jesus' life, death and resurrection, the first Christians are faced with the challenge of translating their experience into a teaching and practice that can be handed on to future generations. They do not as yet have a template. The following texts from the Acts of the Apostles reveal how the followers of the Way observed the work of the Holy Spirit in different communities. One would expect that baptism would be the first step on the Christian journey (the *hodos*). This is what happens in the communities of Jerusalem and Samaria. However, in Damascus and Caesarea the Holy Spirit is present before the people are baptised. A variation of this sequence is found in Ephesus. These are the relevant texts:

Jerusalem, Acts 2:38 (baptism first): 'Repent and be baptised every one of you in the name of Jesus Christ so that your sins may be forgiven; and you will receive the gift of the Holy Spirit.'

Samaria, Acts 8:14-17 (baptism first): 'Now when the apostles at Jerusalem heard that Samaria had accepted the word of God, they sent Peter and John to them. The two went down and prayed for them that they might receive the Holy Spirit (for as yet the Spirit had not come upon any of them; they had only been baptised in the name of the Lord Jesus). Then Peter and John laid their hands on them, and they received the Holy Spirit.'

Damascus (after Paul's conversion), Acts 9:17-18 (Holy Spirit first): 'Ananias went and entered the house. He laid his hands on Saul and said, "Brother Saul, the Lord Jesus, who appeared to you on your way here, has sent me so that you may regain your sight and be filled with the Holy Spirit.'

Caesarea (Peter and Cornelius), Acts 10:44-8 (Holy Spirit first): 'While Peter was still speaking, the Holy Spirit fell upon all who heard the word. The circumcised believers who had come with Peter were astounded that the gift of the Holy Spirit had been poured out even on the Gentiles, for they heard them speaking in tongues and extolling God. Then Peter said, "Can anyone withhold the water for baptising these people who have received the Holy Spirit just as we have?" So he ordered them to be baptised in the name of Jesus Christ.'

Ephesus, Acts 19:1-6 (John's baptism; Christian baptism; Holy Spirit): 'While Apollos was in Corinth, Paul passed through the inland regions and came to Ephesus, where he found some disciples. He said to them, "Did you receive the Holy Spirit when you became believers?" They replied, "No, we have not even heard that there is a Holy Spirit." Then he said, "Into what then were you baptised?" They answered,

"Into John's baptism." Paul said, "John baptised with the baptism of repentance, telling the people to believe in the one who was to come after him, that is, in Jesus." On hearing this, they were baptised in the name of the Lord Jesus. When Paul had laid his hands on them, the Holy Spirit came upon them, and they spoke in tongues and prophesied.'

What is evident in these texts is that the Spirit acts freely and is not limited to the actions of the apostles. The Holy Spirit is present in the baptised, though this is not obvious in each case cited. The laying on of hands precipitates the coming of the Spirit. This is a gesture that is present (*mutatis mutandis*) in the other sacraments too. In the Mass this is called the *epiclesis*, when the priest extends his hands over the bread and wine just before the institution narrative. The Holy Spirit is active in every sacrament.

Thomas Marsh (1932–94) interprets the evidence from the Acts of the Apostles as supporting the view that there were two rites from the beginning:

[B]aptism and forgiveness of sins are consistently related together, whereas the gift of the Spirit is just as consistently presented as distinct and separate from baptism. Indeed, in those key passages where Luke describes the *full* process of Christian initiation, Acts 8:12-17 [Samaria]; 19:1-7 [Ephesus], the gift of the Spirit is an effect of a post-baptismal rite, imposition of the hands. We are therefore justified in viewing the gift of the Spirit referred to in this text as an event envisaged as occurring after baptism.[14]

From the years 100 to 200 there is no evidence of a second sacrament, at least not in the main documents from this period: the *Didache*, the *Letter of Barnabas*, the *Apology* of Justin. In the third century we find different ceremonies within the one rite of baptism, e.g. the laying on of hands, the anointing and the signing (*sphragis*). Initiation involved baptism and Eucharist only. We find this pattern in the writings of Hippolytus of Rome, Origen of Alexandria (*c*.185–*c*.254) and Tertullian.

Two historical factors paved the way for a gradual change in the way baptism was celebrated. The first was the deurbanisation of Christianity.

As Christian communities grew in rural areas, baptism was performed by *presbuteroi* (priests), with the final anointing and laying on of hands being reserved to the bishop. This occurred much later than the baptism. The norm of reserving the 'final part of the baptism rite' to the bishop goes back to the synod held at Elvira (Granada) around the year 300. The reason for the imposition of hands by the bishop dates back to St Cyprian of Carthage in the third century, who based his argument on the practice recorded in Acts 8:14-17 (Samaria). But from the fourth to the sixth centuries a separation of rites began to occur. It was further accelerated by the growing practice of infant baptism, whereby the anointing and laying on of hands by the bishop was delayed until a later age. Confirmation, so understood, also took on the aspect of a mature profession of faith and the anointing was seen as becoming a 'soldier of Christ'. Today, we would prefer to use a less military term, such as one proposed by Pope Francis: we become 'missionary disciples'. What began as a practical adjustment of baptism gradually became a second sacrament.

The initiation of a Christian adult is a process involving three sacraments: baptism, confirmation and Eucharist. This sequence underlines how baptism is incomplete until confirmation has been received. Even in the case of the apostles their initiation came in stages. Prior to the ascension they had grace and some share of the Holy Spirit, but at Pentecost they received the Spirit in a new way to enable them to enter into the new responsibility that was being laid upon them. Confirmation is for each Christian what Pentecost was for the apostolic Church. It gives the Holy Spirit to Christians in a new way, especially the gifts of the Spirit, to enable them to carry out their responsibilities within the Christian Church. Confirmation, then, is about accepting our responsibility for others in that plan of God and so receiving the graces and gifts of the Holy Spirit that we need for that task. The Holy Spirit comes to us in baptism for ourselves, to enable us to become part of God's life and family. The Spirit is given to us in confirmation not just for ourselves but also for others. We become missionary disciples. In summary, with baptism we are recipients of the Holy Spirit; in confirmation we are channels of the Holy Spirit to others. Of course, discussion of the sacraments of initiation must never lose sight of the Eucharist as the goal of the process. For this reason, the rightful place for the celebration of confirmation is Mass.

During the Covid-19 pandemic bishops wisely delegated their priests to celebrate the sacrament outside of Mass, but that was an exceptional circumstance.

GIFTS AND FRUITS OF THE SPIRIT

The seven gifts of the Spirit are based on the text from the prophet, Isaiah:

> A shoot shall come out from the stock of Jesse, and a branch shall grow out of his roots. The spirit of the Lord shall rest on him, the spirit of wisdom and understanding, the spirit of counsel and might, the spirit of knowledge and the fear of the Lord. His delight shall be in the fear of the Lord. (Is 11:1-3)

We list the gifts of the Spirit as follows: wisdom, understanding, good judgement, courage, knowledge, reverence, and wonder and awe in God's presence. In an RCIA programme, or in a class of school children preparing for confirmation, it is useful to discuss the gifts individually and practically. Children invariably start with 'courage'. They will need courage in the future as they grow into the adult world.

The fruits of the Holy Spirit are listed by St Paul: 'The fruit of the Spirit is love, joy, peace, patience, kindness, goodness, trustfulness, gentleness and self-control' (Gal 5:22-3). Preparation for the sacrament could profitably focus on anticipating these fruits and our need for them, both as individuals and as a community.

CONCLUSION

It is essential to point out that these two sacraments are permanent. We can't be 'unbaptised' or 'unconfirmed'. However, they can remain dormant, just like a gift that is unopened and left to gather dust on a shelf. We need to renew our reception of these sacraments. We are given the opportunity to renew our baptism when the rite of sprinkling of holy water is used for the penitential rite or when the Creed is replaced with a renewal of our baptismal promises (e.g. at Easter). But confirmation can often remain on the shelf. Regular renewal of that sacrament would transform our Christian lives. One possibility is to have a vigil for the feast of Pentecost similar to the Easter Vigil.

The Jerusalem community in Paris have such a ceremony on the eve of Pentecost in their church, Saint Gervais. A number of texts from the Old and New Testaments in relation to the Spirit are proclaimed and the congregation is given the opportunity to renew their confirmation. This includes a renewal of the baptismal promises.

One consequence of these two sacraments of initiation is that those who receive them become part of the priesthood of Christ. This will be dealt with in our chapter on priesthood.

Notes

1   *Rite of Christian Initiation of Adults*, Chicago: Liturgy Training Publications, 1988, p. 3, n. 4.

2   See Cornelius Ernst, *The Theology of Grace* ('Theology Today' series 17), Dublin and Cork: Mercier Press, 1974; John Hardon SJ, *History and Theology of Grace*, Michigan: Veritas Press of Ave Maria College, 2002; Roger Haight, *The Experience and Language of Grace*, New York: Paulist Press, 1979; art. 'Grace' in F.L. Cross and E.A. Livingstone (eds), *The Oxford Dictionary of the Christian Church*, 2nd edn, Oxford: Oxford University Press, 1957, pp. 697–8; Martin Henry, 'Reflections on Grace', 1, 2, 3, *Irish Theological Quarterly*, Vol. 66, No. 3 (2001), pp. 195– 210, Vol. 66, No. 4 (2001), pp. 295–314, Vol. 67, No. 1 (2002), pp. 55–68.

3   See also Gal 1:15–16; 1 Cor 15:10; Rm 1:5; 12:3.

4   Ernst, *The Theology of Grace*, p. 19.

5   Regis A. Duffy, 'Baptism and Confirmation', in Francis Schüssler Fiorenza and John P. Galvin (eds) *Systematic Theology: Roman Catholic Perspectives* Volume II, Minneapolis: Fortress Press, 1991, p. 220.

6   World Council of Churches, *Baptism, Eucharist and Ministry* (Faith and Order Paper, no. 111), Geneva: World Council of Churches, 1982.

7   Duffy, 'Baptism and Confirmation', p. 221.

8   Vatican II, *Lumen Gentium*, 1964, 7.

9   Ibid., 11.

10 Vatican II, *Presbyterorum Ordinis*, 1965, 2.

11 Vatican II, *Unitatis Redintegratio*, 1964, 22.

12 St Thomas Aquinas, *Summa Theologiae*, IIIa, q. 73, a. 3, Respondeo.

13 See Duffy, 'Baptism and Confirmation', pp. 227–8.

14 Thomas A. Marsh, *Gift of Community: Baptism and Confirmation*, Wilmington, Delaware: Michael Glazier Inc., 1984, p. 53.

CHAPTER FOUR

SACRAMENTS OF CHRISTIAN INITIATION II: THE EUCHARIST

CENTRALITY OF THE MASS IN A POST-PANDEMIC CHURCH

Since the beginning of the Covid-19 pandemic, religions have experienced a dramatic change in their life and practice. For long periods churches were closed. Then there was an ebb and flow of access: hubs of fifty could attend Mass and services; at times the liturgy was live-streamed only; no more than ten people could attend a funeral; only six guests were allowed at a wedding. Christmas 2020 was like no other; Christmas 2021 was marginally better. Though greater improvements were seen at Christmas in 2022, this was yet a far cry from the vibrant Christmas celebrations when people came in their thousands, even if they had not been to church all year. So where does all this leave us as a church? Will live-streaming be the norm into the future? Many say they prefer Mass online; they claim to pay more heed to the readings as they listen over a cup of coffee. And then there is the option of liturgical tourism; one can try out other parishes at the click of a mouse.

Just before leaving office, Archbishop Diarmuid Martin claimed that, in his opinion, many people would not return to church services after the Covid-19 pandemic. If this is true, then that has serious consequences for the place of liturgy and sacraments in the Christian life. Televised and live-streamed services have been a most welcome interim solution when attendance at Mass was not possible. But in the long term will it have undermined our appreciation of the Eucharist as a community experience, culminating in the reception of Holy Communion? Pope Francis has drawn attention to this danger and discontinued his practice of broadcasting daily Mass. I am not advocating the discontinuation of live-streaming liturgies. On the contrary, I believe it will continue to be much appreciated by people who are unable to go to church. For funeral services, it enables family members and friends to be virtually present from all over the world.

Jesus refers to himself as bread: 'I am the living bread that came down from heaven. Whoever eats of this bread will live forever; and the bread that I shall give for the life of the world is my flesh' (Jn 6:51). This is not a spiritual communion only. We are familiar with the prayer of spiritual communion in our live-streamed Masses. But Jesus intends us to eat the bread of life in a physical way. St John appreciated that because he uses a very physical term for 'to eat' (*trogein*); it really means to chew/to bite, and it is not the usual verb for eating in Greek (*phagein*). We can take from this that Jesus intended us to consume the bread of life physically and not just spiritually. In addition, we can say that the climax of the Mass is the reception of Holy Communion and not the words of institution. It is the whole eucharistic prayer that is consecratory and not just the words of institution. So, we have a huge challenge in convincing our people that to participate fully in the Eucharist we need to receive Communion. Coupled with that challenge is the state of belief in the real presence.

The second major issue that arises in our time from seeing online Masses as complete eucharistic experiences in themselves is the fact that the community dimension is missing; it is an individualistic devotion. Allied to this is the consequences of being a eucharistic people. The Eucharist doesn't end with the *Ita Missa Est* ('the Mass is ended'). In some ways this marks the beginning, not the end.

This chapter on the Eucharist has an added contemporary relevance given the experience of recent years. We never thought we would see the day when the obligation to attend Sunday Mass would be lifted. Now we are faced with the challenge of re-establishing the centrality of weekly Eucharist in Christian life. It is hoped that we can do so in a positive way, not relying on fear as was the case when I was growing up. This chapter aims to address this contemporary situation by showing the richness of the Eucharist and its necessity for living a full Christian life. We begin by examining some conciliar and post-conciliar documents.

THE EUCHARIST AS SOURCE AND SUMMIT

The twentieth century has been called the century of the Church, with the Vatican Council as the Council of the Church. Two major documents on the Church were issued by the Council: *Lumen Gentium* and *Gaudium et Spes*. The document on the liturgy, *Sacrosanctum Concilium*, was the first document to be published, on 4 December 1963. Major work had been done on the liturgy prior to the Council by people like Dom Odo Casel OSB (1886–1948) and Emile Mersch SJ (1890–1940).

The document on the liturgy dealt all too briefly with the Eucharist. What it did was highlight its importance with little further elucidation: 'The liturgy is the summit towards which the activity of the Church is directed; it is also the font from which all her power flows.'[1] A similar statement is to be found in two other documents of the Council. *Lumen Gentium* describes the Eucharist as the 'source and summit of the entire Christian life.'[2] *Christus Dominus* (Decree on the Pastoral Office of Bishops in the Church) varies the phraseology somewhat: 'To accomplish their task of sanctification, the parish priests will see to it that the celebration of the eucharistic sacrifice will be the centre and summit of the entire life of the Christian community.'[3] Pope John Paul II, in his encyclical on the Eucharist, *Ecclesia de Eucharistia*, uses similar language: 'The Church draws her life from the Eucharist. This truth does not simply express a daily experience of faith, but recapitulates *the heart of the mystery of the Church*'; '*The Church draws her life from Christ in the Eucharist*'; 'The Eucharist, which is in an outstanding way the sacrament of the paschal mystery, *stands at the centre of the Church's life*.'[4] Pope Benedict XVI again uses similar language: 'In every age of the Church's history the eucharistic celebration, as the source and summit of her life and mission, shines forth in the liturgical rite in all its richness and variety.'[5] The idea of the Eucharist as summit of the Christian life is found too in the *Summa Theologiae*. As we read in the previous chapter, St Thomas Aquinas describes baptism as the 'beginning of the spiritual life' and the Eucharist as the 'summit of the spiritual life, and the goal of all the sacraments'.[6]

These are tightly packed statements. I will draw on three post-conciliar documents that attempt to go some distance in complementing the writings of the Council itself:

1. Pope John Paul II, *Ecclesia de Eucharistia*, 17 April 2003 (encyclical);
2. Pope John Paul II, *Mane Nobiscum Domine*, 7 October 2004 (apostolic letter);
3. Pope Benedict XVI, *Sacramentum Caritatis*, 13 March 2007 (apostolic exhortation).

Why these documents some forty years after the publication of *Sacrosanctum Concilium*? The first reason is to deepen the import of the Vatican Council. An ecumenical council cannot do everything: it is the beginning of a process and not the definitive fruit of the deliberations of the Fathers. The second reason why these documents have appeared in the first decade of the twenty-first century is the crumbling of Christian culture in so many countries in the West. A new and thorough catechesis is required. I would like to quote Archbishop Jean-Louis Bruges OP (b. 1943), a moral theologian, commenting on the situation in the secularised, post-Christian West:

> People no longer know how to read Christian art. They no longer know how to understand the discourse of the Church, especially when it treats of moral questions; the same is true of its rites and way of life. The Christian era is only interpreted in caricatures and simplistic visions fed through films, television programmes and newspaper articles.[7]

There is much truth in this statement. The discourse of the Church is seen as just another voice in a chorus of discourses. Church authority has been deleted in a culture of tolerance.

The third reason why these recent documents on the Eucharist are so important is the openness that is to be found in many young people.

The ground is fertile. The younger generation knows that it doesn't know. There is a promising generosity among the young who want to learn. This is especially evident in the catechesis that accompanies the World Youth Days. The new generation is largely free of the prejudices of their elders and is more open. This is a grace and an immense task. We need to rebuild. So what is in these documents? We will begin by focusing on the encyclical *Ecclesia de Eucharistia*, from 2003, which is rich and relevant to our subject.

THE EUCHARIST AS SACRIFICE AND COMMUNION

Pope John Paul II draws attention to three critical issues in relation to the Eucharist: the centrality of sacrifice, the necessity of the ministerial priesthood and the horizontal reduction of the Eucharist to a form of proclamation. This is how he launches his encyclical in 2003:

> Stripped of its sacrificial meaning, it is celebrated as if it were simply a fraternal banquet. Furthermore, the necessity of the ministerial priesthood, grounded in apostolic succession, is at times obscured and the sacramental nature of the Eucharist is reduced to its mere effectiveness as a form of proclamation.[8]

The first issue is the question of the Mass as sacrifice. When the Mass is reduced to the horizontal level, a banquet, it loses its focus and meaning. The fact that it is Christ's sacrifice offered to the Father, in which we are privileged to participate, has sometimes been blurred since the Council.

The second point raised by Pope John Paul II is the undermining of the ministerial priesthood and failure to see it as essential to the Eucharist. The Eucharist is the principal reason for the sacrament of orders.

Finally, Pope John Paul II sees the danger of a horizontal reductionism whereby the liturgy becomes flat-footed and a theological lowest common denominator prevails. The word overshadows the eucharistic sacrifice. Horizontal reductionism is evident in a Eucharist where the Liturgy of the Word dominates. In an effort to make the Mass more accessible to an increasingly uneducated congregation – theologically – there is a danger of reducing the language and symbolism to banalities, omitting such rich terminology as grace, Trinity, divine and, especially, sacrifice. When the salt becomes tasteless, 'let us proclaim the mystery of faith'. Where is the mystery? We need to rediscover the mystery that is the Eucharist.

Two extremes in particular need to be avoided. The Eucharist understood as communion alone risks becoming just a fellowship meal. The link with Christ and the paschal mystery becomes clouded. The status of the sacramental elements (the consecrated bread and wine) is blurred. This is the extreme of horizontal reductionism.

The second extreme to be avoided is the separation of sacrifice from communion. The Eucharist understood uniquely as sacrifice runs the risk of individualism, with no community dimension. Here the congregation is a spectator at the action of the priest. Remember the Eucharist is 'my sacrifice and yours', in the words of the *Orate Fratres*. The Eucharist is not sacrifice alone, nor is it communion alone. I propose that it is communion because it is sacrifice, and it is sacrifice because it is communion. Sacrifice and communion are not two stages in the liturgy. Now we examine more closely what we mean by sacrifice.

WHAT IS SACRIFICE?

We struggle to understand the idea of sacrifice. We tend to see it through the lens of pagan religions that offered sacrifices to appease an angry god, or gods. A superficial judgement of Jewish sacrifice is marred by a similar view of sacrifice, that it is aimed at keeping God on our side to ensure a good harvest and success in war. But Jewish sacrifice was not always selfish and utilitarian. There was an inner dimension to it that sought union with God: sacrifice was selfless worship. It was a constant struggle, especially on the part of the prophets, to purify the intentions of those who offered sacrifice. This is cryptically expressed by the Lord through the prophet Hosea: 'For I desire steadfast love and not sacrifice, the knowledge of God rather than burnt offerings' (Hos 6:6).

External sacrifices are of no value unless they are accompanied by an inner attitude of love. This implies that sacrifices cannot be isolated moments in a life of selfishness. There must be a consistency between the way we live and the sacrifice we offer. This is expressed in a memorable way by St Paul: 'I appeal to you therefore, brothers and sisters, by the mercies of God, to present your bodies as a living sacrifice, holy and acceptable to God, which is your spiritual worship' (Rm 12:1). In other words, the whole of life is a sacrifice to God. This does not mean that it is necessarily a deprivation or a negative experience. In a word, it is a life of love. St Thérèse of Lisieux (1873–97) found her vocation as love in the heart of the Church.[9] This is the meaning of Romans 12:1. It is sacrifice and it is communion. St Augustine's understanding of sacrifice in *The City of God* further elucidates what Thérèse discovered in her prayer:

> The true sacrifice is offered in every act which is designed to unite us to God in a holy fellowship, every act, that is, which is directed to that final good which makes possible our true felicity.[10]

Sacrifice and love are synonymous. This is true *par excellence* in the passion and death of Christ. Pope John Paul II expresses it like this:

> The gift of his love and obedience to the point of giving his life (cf. Jn 10:17-18) is in the first place a gift to his Father. Certainly it is a gift given for our sake, and indeed that of all humanity (cf. Mt 26:28; Mk 14:24; Lk 22:20; Jn 10:15), yet it is *first and foremost a gift to the Father*.[11]

This is not a sacrifice to placate an angry God but a loving self-giving to the One who is love. St Augustine emphasised that God's love for us did not come about as a result of his Son's sacrifice but was always there: 'The Father loved us previously, not only before his Son died for us but also before he founded the world.'[12] This evokes St Paul's words: 'But God proves his love for us in that while we still were sinners Christ died for us' (Rm 5:8). The unity expressed between the Father and the Son on Calvary is the sacrament of the unity between humanity and God and, in turn, our communion with each other. This love and sacrifice is truly present whenever the Eucharist is celebrated. For this reason we can state that the Eucharist is sacrifice because it is communion and it is communion because it is sacrifice. Now we attempt to answer the question as to the relationship between the sacrifice of the cross and the Eucharist. We do so by first looking at the relationship between the Last Supper and the Passion.

ANTICIPATION AND REMEMBRANCE

At the Last Supper the sacrifice of the cross is anticipated and present in the sacramental presence and self-giving in the upper room. *Ecclesia de Eucharistia* expresses it in these terms: 'The institution of the Eucharist sacramentally anticipated the events which were about to take place'.[13] Further:

> Jesus did not simply state that what he was giving them to eat and drink was his body and his blood; he also expressed *its sacrificial meaning* and made sacramentally present his sacrifice which would soon be offered on the Cross for the salvation of all.[14]

In this way Jesus enabled his apostles to participate in the passion in the most intimate way. By eating the consecrated bread and wine they were actually consuming the sacrifice of love on the cross. They were part of the love and sacrifice of Jesus to his Father. What happened on the following day was sacramentally anticipated at the Last Supper.

To appreciate more fully the significance of the Last Supper and of our Eucharist today we would do well to read the institution narratives in the New Testament:

---

1 Corinthians 11:23-6

For I received from the Lord what I also handed on to you, that the Lord Jesus on the night when he was betrayed took a loaf of bread, and when he had given thanks, he broke it and said, 'This is my body that is FOR YOU. DO THIS IN REMEMBRANCE OF ME.' In the same way he took the cup also, after supper, saying, 'This cup is the **new covenant** in my blood. DO THIS, as often as you drink it, IN REMEMBRANCE OF ME.' For as often as you eat this bread and drink the cup, you proclaim the Lord's death until he comes.

Luke 22:19-20

Then he took a loaf of bread, and when he had given thanks, he broke it and gave it to them, saying, 'This is my body, which is given FOR YOU. DO THIS IN REMEMBRANCE OF ME.' And he did the same with the cup after supper, saying, 'This cup that is poured out for you is the **new covenant** in my blood.

Mark 14:22-4

<u>While they were eating</u>, he took a loaf of bread, and after blessing it he broke it, gave it to them, and said, 'TAKE; this is my body.' Then he took a cup, and after giving thanks he gave it to them, and all of them drank from it. He said to them, 'This is my blood of the **covenant**, which is *poured out for many.*'

Matthew 26:26-8

<u>While they were eating</u>, Jesus took a loaf of bread, and after blessing it he broke it, gave it to the disciples, and said, 'TAKE, eat; this is my body.' Then he took a cup, and after giving thanks he gave it to them, saying, 'Drink from it, all of you; for this is my blood of the **covenant**, which is *poured out for many <u>for the forgiveness of sins</u>.*'

The similarities and differences between the four accounts enrich our appreciation and understanding of this great mystery of our faith. Whether the term is 'covenant' (Mark and Matthew), or 'new covenant' (Paul and Luke), the institution narratives recall the sacrifice of Moses in Exodus establishing a new covenant with the people. Paul and Luke use the phrase 'for you', which could refer simply to the disciples present but more likely it refers to all who would come after them. Mark and Matthew use the expression 'for many', which is a Semitic expression for a great multitude, a countless number. It is equivalent in our language to mean 'for all'. The fact that the new translation of the *Roman Missal* uses the term 'for many' in place of the previously used term 'for all' is more faithful to scripture, but the meaning hasn't changed. Only Matthew proposes the forgiveness of sins as the reason for the sacrifice of Christ. Interestingly, this Matthean phrase has become part of our eucharistic prayers. Of prime importance is the command of Jesus to 'do this in remembrance of me' (Paul and Luke): it is the reason why we celebrate the Eucharist ever since. We now turn to the significance of 'remembrance' in our liturgies.

The Last Supper anticipated the death and resurrection of Jesus. In our celebrations of the Eucharist the sacrifice of Calvary is present in the memorial: 'Do this in remembrance of me,' understood in the light of Jewish ritual memorial, especially the Passover as the ritual memorial of the Exodus. We are aware of the criticism levelled at Catholics accusing us of making Christ suffer and die every time we celebrate Mass. St John Chrysostom was aware of the difficulties that might arise when the relationship between the one sacrifice of Christ and subsequent celebrations of the Eucharist might be questioned. He wrote: 'We offer always the same [Sacrifice], or rather we perform a remembrance of a sacrifice.'[15] The Jewish understanding of memory in relation to the Passover as memorial of the Exodus enables us to express the idea of the Eucharist as sacrifice.

The Exodus was the series of events, usually dated around 1250 BCE, by which the Jewish people were rescued from the slavery of Egypt and began their great journey through the desert that led to the Promised Land, Israel. According to the faith of the Bible, the principal agent of this rescue was God himself, and this series of events is foundational for Jewish faith. In the Bible God is the Lord of history. As a result, there is a sense in which every generation of the chosen people is involved in what happens at the Exodus.

THE PASSOVER SEDER

The Passover is the feast in which these events of long ago are celebrated annually, the Seder being the principal ritual of Passover. The Jews regard it as the great feast of their liberation by God from the darkness of evil. In other words, it celebrates their redemption. In this way the feast is a renewal of union with God and an entering into the graces and blessings of the Exodus once again. Through the liturgy they express their sense of all their people having been involved in the original events. On the individual level, the Seder requires every participant to feel as though he or she has personally left Egypt. In the Book of Deuteronomy we find the exhortation: 'Remember that you were a slave in Egypt' (Deut 16:12). And again: 'We were Pharaoh's slaves in Egypt, but the Lord brought us out of Egypt with a mighty hand' (Deut 6:21).

The Passover has been established as a 'memorial' of the Exodus: 'This day shall be a day of remembrance for you' (Ex 12:14; 13:3, 16). From what we have seen it is clear that memory, memorial and commemoration can have a very special meaning when they are found in Jewish liturgy. It is not just a question of calling to mind an event from the past, but of bringing into our world the reality of that past event. An essential part of the Passover Seder is recounting in detail the event of the Exodus. This retelling of the story is called the Haggadah. It makes clear that the family celebrating the event has itself been saved from slavery in Egypt: 'We were slaves to Pharaoh in Egypt, but Hashem our God took us out from there with a mighty hand and an outstretched arm.'[16]

Just as the Passover is the living memorial of the Exodus, so is the Eucharist the living memorial of Christ's death and resurrection. Christ refers to his death by speaking of his body given and his blood poured out. Just as the Exodus was made present by the Jews in their celebration of the Passover, so the events of Christ's death and resurrection are made present by Christians in their celebration of the Eucharist.

The application of Jewish ritual memorial to our understanding of the Eucharist has led to a dramatic breakthrough in the field of contemporary ecumenical relations. This biblical theology of memorial is something that was worked out by Catholic and Protestant scholars alike once they began to explore the Jewish background to our New Testament texts. At the time of the Reformation, one could say that Catholic and Protestant theology of the Eucharist had been divided by the word 'memory'. Protestants said that the Eucharist was only a memorial, meaning that it is only a calling to mind of the past. Catholics said it was more than memory because it was a sacrifice. The modern theology of memorial enables us to say the Eucharist is sacrifice because it is memorial. We must not give the impression that all problems on this point have been solved, but the rediscovery of the Jewish sense of memorial has placed the whole discussion on a new plane and made possible a coming closer in a way that previously would have seemed inconceivable.

It is important to see the unity of the Eucharist and the cross, which builds on the notion of real presence. In the Eucharist there is a real presence of Christ's body and blood. But as well as that real presence of his body given and his blood poured out, there is a real presence of the action by which that body was given and that blood was poured out. Christ's sacrifice is really present. The Eucharist is a sacrifice in so far as there is eucharistic change. If there was no eucharistic change, it would be fitting to call the Eucharist an empty memorial. If host and cup were only signs of Christ's body and blood, the celebration would only be a sign, a mental evocation of the cross. But in the Eucharist something happens: Christ lays down on the altar his very body and his very blood. He gives not just a sign of himself but his very self. Jesus giving himself is the kernel of what happened on the cross and it is the kernel of what happens in the Mass.

So many different means have been used to express this truth, the most renowned being that of St Thomas Aquinas who used the philosophy of Aristotle to expound the mystery. He distinguished between the binaries matter and form, substance and accident to express the idea that while the material elements of the sacrament look the same, a new reality is brought about. If the bread were tested in a laboratory before and after Mass it would have the same chemical properties; its form or accident is unchanged. It is the substance that is new, and Aquinas proposed the term 'transubstantiation' to evoke that change of substance. The Council of Trent formally declared this to be the teaching of the Church and Pope John Paul II reaffirmed it in *Ecclesia de Eucharistia*.[17]

THE EUCHARIST AS MYSTERY OF LIGHT
Following the encyclical *Ecclesia de Eucharistia* in 2003, Pope John Paul II proclaimed a Year of the Eucharist from October 2004 to October 2005. To mark the beginning of that year he published the apostolic letter *Mane Nobiscum Domine* ('Stay with us, Lord'). This letter is a reflection based on Luke 24, the road to Emmaus story. This short letter reveals once again the contemplative spirit of the ageing Pope and his preoccupation with the importance of rediscovering the mystery of the Eucharist. In this letter he describes the Eucharist as a mystery of light but says that it is pre-eminently a *mysterium fidei* ('a mystery of faith').[18] Jesus describes himself as the 'light of the world' (Jn 8:12), and this quality clearly appears at those moments in his life, like the transfiguration and the resurrection, in which his divine glory shines forth. Yet the Pope says that in the Eucharist the glory of Christ remains veiled. It is from within that mystery of faith that Christ reveals himself: 'Through the mystery of his complete hiddenness, Christ becomes a mystery of light, thanks to which believers are led into the depths of the divine life.'[19] We see here the paradox of revelation: revelation is at once an opening up, an unveiling, and, at the same time, it is a further veiling of the mystery. And the divine life, to which Pope John Paul II refers, is the community of the Father, Son and Holy Spirit. The Pope refers to Rublev's icon of the Trinity, which places the Eucharist at the centre of the life of the Trinity, a remarkable intuition on the part of the artist.

The Eucharist is light because at every Mass the Liturgy of the Word precedes the Liturgy of the Eucharist in the unity of the two 'tables', the table of the Word and the table of the Bread. We see immediately how the Emmaus story is an archetype of the Eucharist: the people gather preoccupied with their own affairs, just like the two disciples with their faces downcast after the events of Good Friday. Jesus joins them; he is present in the people gathered. He explains the scriptures to them and their hearts burn within them. This corresponds to our Liturgy of the Word, where the homily plays an important role in opening up the assembly to the wonder that is about to happen. Then the disciples have their eyes opened and they recognise him in the breaking of bread (Lk 24:35). They recognise him because they had been prepared by Jesus on the way: their minds were enlightened as he explained the scriptures and their hearts were enkindled. Because of this, the sign spoke to them at the table: it became a sacrament. The Pope says that through these signs the mystery opens up before the eyes of the believer. He recalls what he had said in *Ecclesia de Eucharistia*, that we are constantly tempted to reduce the Eucharist to our own dimensions, while in reality *'it is we who must open ourselves up to the dimensions of the Mystery'*.[20]

I should like to take another text for a moment to draw out further the implication of the Eucharist as the mystery of light. This is an extract from a sermon on the ascension by Pope St Leo the Great where he comments on Luke 24:

> It was during this time that the Lord joined the two disciples as their companion on the road; and by rebuking them for their timid and fearful hesitation he dispelled the darkness of doubt *from all our minds*. Their enlightened hearts received the flame of faith; cool before, they glowed when the Lord *unfolded* the scriptures to them. As they ate with him, their eyes were opened in the breaking of bread – opened much more happily to the revealed *glory of our nature* than were the eyes of the first members of our race who were filled with shame at their sins.[21]

The disciples moved from darkness to light, the darkness of doubt and fear to the light of recognition and certainty. But St Leo claims the doubt is removed 'from all our minds'. The embers of faith were enkindled by the Word as Christ explained the scriptures to them: 'Were not our hearts burning within us ... ?' (Lk 24:32). Leo uses the verb 'unfolded', evocative of revelation. Luke 24 highlights how the disciples recognised him at the breaking of bread, Leo goes further when he says that they saw the revealed glory 'of our nature'. He contrasts the joy and happiness of the two disciples at seeing their own nature in a new light with the shame of Adam and Eve. Here Leo is evoking all that is meant by the idea of the new creation and the new man, as found in St Paul's writings and in the Book of Revelation. Pope Benedict XVI expresses this idea when he calls for a mystagogical catechesis:

> The mature fruit of mystagogy is an awareness that one's life is being progressively transformed by the holy mysteries being celebrated. The aim of all Christian education, moreover, is to train the believer in an adult faith that can make him a 'new creation', capable of bearing witness in his surroundings to the Christian hope that inspires him.[22]

It is in their encounter with the risen Christ in the Eucharist that these disciples discover who they are as human beings destined to union with God. This is not a static condition but one that is continually in a state of transformation as we are configured to Christ.

This is a major insight. The mystery of the Eucharist opens up for us the mystery that we are ourselves. It is a very well-established understanding going back through the tradition, whereby all revelation of God is a revelation of man to himself. This is highlighted in *Gaudium et Spes*: 'In the Incarnate Word, both the mystery of God and the mystery of man are revealed.'[23]

THE EUCHARIST AS SACRAMENT OF LOVE

The Vatican Council document on the liturgy, *Sacrosanctum Concilium*, has a summary statement on the Eucharist that brings together, in a cogent way, the different aspects of this mystery:

> At the Last Supper, on the night he was betrayed, our Saviour instituted the eucharistic *sacrifice* of his Body and Blood. This he did in order to perpetuate the sacrifice of the Cross throughout the ages until he should come again, and so to entrust to his beloved Spouse, the Church, a *memorial* of his death and resurrection: a *sacrament of love*, a sign of

unity, a bond of charity, a paschal banquet in which Christ is consumed, the soul is filled with *grace*, and a pledge of *future glory* is given to us.[24]

In addition to the aspects of the Eucharist we have already considered, I should like to reflect on two further aspects, namely the Eucharist as a sacrament of love and as a pledge of future glory.

Celebration of the Eucharist is not a disembodied exercise: it must take account of what is happening in the community. The early Eucharists, as recounted in the Acts of the Apostles, knew how to connect liturgy and life. There was never anyone in want in their communities (see, in particular, Acts 4:32-5). St John Chrysostom has a startling reflection that links the Eucharist to Matthew 25 (the judgement):

> Would you honour the body of Christ? Do not despise his nakedness; do not honour him here in church clothed in silk vestments and then pass him by unclothed and frozen outside. Remember that he who said, 'This is my body', and made good his words, also said, 'You saw me hungry and gave me no food', and, 'in so far as you did it not to one of these, you did it not to me'. In the first sense the body of Christ does not need clothing but worship from a pure heart. In the second sense it does need clothing and all the care we can give it.[25]

In practice, this means that our parishes need to be communities of care, especially for the weakest. We cannot talk about celebrating the Eucharist without giving equal regard to love of neighbour. In the early centuries of the Church the care of the poor was in the hands of the deacons. Then, as deacons were subsumed into the presbyterate, the monasteries performed that role. In more recent times, the Vincent de Paul Society and other church-based organisations take responsibility for those in need. That is as it should be. But there are so many who are poor in non-materialistic ways who need to be the focus of our eucharistic care. One of the motivations inspiring this book is that catechetics in all its guises is a priority where the spiritually needy are concerned.

Quoting from his address to the Roman Curia in December 2005, Pope Benedict XVI gives great weight to the human relationships that should result from the Eucharist:

> And it is precisely this personal encounter with the Lord that then strengthens the social mission contained in the Eucharist, which seeks to break down not only the walls that separate the Lord and ourselves, *but also and especially* the walls that separate us from one another.[26]

How we treat each other is at the heart of the relationship between Eucharist and the community.

A PLEDGE OF FUTURE GLORY

An essential aspect of the Eucharist is that it anticipates the end time, when all things are recapitulated in Christ (Eph 1:10). So far, in this chapter, we have focused on the Eucharist as remembrance of the death and resurrection of Christ, using memory as a making present here and now. But the Eucharist also concerns the future. The love/sacrifice in which we participate anticipates our union in the life of the Trinity. This begins at baptism and is complete at the end of time. Pope Benedict XVI has an apt summary of that aspect of the Eucharist:

> Jesus showed that he wished to transfer to the entire community which he had founded the task of being, within history, the sign and instrument of the eschatological gathering that had its origin in him. Consequently, every eucharistic celebration sacramentally accomplishes the eschatological gathering of the People of God.[27]

The continuation between life here and life hereafter is teased out by Henri de Lubac in terms of image and likeness:

> For the Fathers of the Church, man, created in the image of God, that is to say, with those divine prerogatives of reason, freedom, immortality, and dominion by right over nature, was made in view of his likeness to God, who is the perfection of this image. This means that he is destined to

82

live eternally in God, to enter into the internal movement
of the Trinitarian Life and to take all creation with him.[28]

De Lubac's phrase describing likeness as entering the internal movement
of the Trinitarian life is incredibly rich. The Trinity is a community of
love where the divine Persons are in a relationship of movement. The
traditional term for the relationships within the Trinity is *perichoresis*
(Latin: *circumincessio*), which tries to capture the dynamic life of God.[29]
The Trinitarian life of love is not static but active, a reality too infrequently
captured in our language and contemporary biblical translations.

In *The Splendor of the Church*, de Lubac connects the possibility of
participation in the life of the Trinity with the sacrifice of Christ: 'He
made us to be brought together into the heart of the life of the Trinity.
Christ offered himself in sacrifice so that we might be one in that unity
of the divine Persons.'[30] Christ not only reveals the Trinity but, through
his sacrifice, he makes it possible for humanity to enter the Trinitarian
life.

So how does all this help us to understand the Eucharist as 'a
sacrament of love, a sign of unity, a bond of charity'? Let's go back to
our Thomistic definition of sacraments: sacraments effect what they
signify (*efficiunt quod figurant*).[31] The Eucharist signifies the mystery
of Trinitarian love: as a sacrament, it brings about that reality. The
Trinitarian community of love is present in the Eucharist, not in a static
way as if we were mere spectators. The truth is rather that we are made
one in the depths of the divine life. Pope Benedict XVI commenting
on this says that the *res* of the sacrament of the Eucharist is the unity
of the faithful: the Eucharist is at the root of the Church as a mystery
of communion.[32]

THE EUCHARIST AND SYNODALITY

As mentioned in the introduction to this book, the three synodal
signposts of participation, communion and mission are also eucharistic
terms. What the Vatican Council document on the liturgy says about
participation in the liturgy implies participation in the whole life of the
Church:

> Mother Church earnestly desires that all the faithful should
> be led to that full, conscious, and active participation in

liturgical celebrations which is demanded by the very nature of the liturgy, and to which the Christian people, 'a chosen race, a royal priesthood, a holy nation, a redeemed people' (1 Pt 2:9, cf. 2:4-5) have a right and obligation by reason of their baptism.[33]

Participation in the liturgy as 'full, conscious, and active' puts paid to the idea that people are mere spectators: the laity celebrate the Mass with the priest, though a ministerial priest is necessary to the sacrament. Pope Francis adds his authority to this view when he states in his apostolic letter *Desiderio Desideravi*: 'Let us always remember that it is the Church, the Body of Christ, that is the celebrating subject and not just the priest.'[34] We have pointed out that the Mass is the source and summit of the Christian life. This surely implies that the laity are meant to have a 'full, conscious, and active' participation in all aspects of Church life.

The second synodal signpost is communion. We have seen in this chapter that communion is brought about by the sacrifice of Christ made present in every Eucharist. This is the source of synodal communion. It is not a mere sociological coming together. Commenting on the 'people of God' model of Church, Walter Kasper (b.1933) distinguishes between *laos tou Theou* and *demos tou Theou*. *Laos* suggests a co-responsibility of all members of the Church for the good of the Church; *demos* connotes a political association, leading to a democratisation of the Church. The latter is a predominant focus of secular commentary when proposing ways in which the Church must change. Kasper comments: 'Unfortunately, this demand [for democratisation] is often linked to ideological goals which aim to eliminate the differences between charisms, ministries and services.'[35] He is drawing attention to the fact that the Church is not a democracy on the lines of a political party. It is a eucharistic people that draws its life from the sacrifice of Christ, exemplified in his self-giving on the cross. For this reason, a synod of the Church is not a *tabula rasa* where decisions can be taken that fail to take account of the will of Christ as revealed in scripture and in the tradition of the Church.

The third synodal signpost is mission. In his encyclical on the Eucharist, Pope John Paul II has this to say:

The Church's mission stands in continuity with the mission of Christ: 'As the Father has sent me, even so I send you' (Jn 20:21). From the perpetuation of the sacrifice of the Cross and her communion with the body and blood of Christ in the Eucharist, the Church draws the spiritual power needed to carry out her mission. The Eucharist thus appears as both *the source* and *the summit* of all evangelisation, since its goal is the communion of mankind with Christ and in him with the Father and the Holy Spirit.[36]

Mission draws its impetus and life from the love and sacrifice of the Eucharist. Mission is not going to be successful based on publicity and persuasion alone – not even by books on sacraments! Effective mission and evangelisation come from the heart of the Church, which is the Eucharist. In the year 2000 the then Cardinal Ratzinger claimed that we need to become Eucharist, proposing St Thérèse of Lisieux as the perfect example of a missionary even though she never left her convent.[37]

Notes

1   Vatican II, *Sacrosanctum Concilium*, 1963, 10.
2   Vatican II, *Lumen Gentium*, 1964, 11.
3   Vatican II, *Christus Dominus*, 1965, 30.
4   Pope John Paul II, *Ecclesia de Eucharistia*, 2003, 1, 6, 3.
5   Pope Benedict XVI, *Sacramentum Caritatis*, 2007, 3.
6   St Thomas Aquinas, *Summa Theologiae*, IIIa, q. 73, a. 3, Respondeo.
7   J.-L. Brugès OP, 'L'eucharistie et l'urgence du mystère', *Nouvelle Revue Théologique*, Vol. 130. No. 1, (2008), p. 5. Translation my own.
8   Pope John Paul II, *Ecclesia de Eucharistia*, 10.
9   Thérèse de Lisieux, *Oeuvres complètes*, Paris: Cerf et Desclée de Brouwer, 1992, Manuscrit B, 225–6.
10 St Augustine, *The City of God*, Bk X, 6.
11 Pope John Paul II, *Ecclesia de Eucharistia*, 13.
12 St Augustine, *De Trinitate* 13.11.15, in Gerald O'Collins and Michael Keenan Jones, *Jesus Our Priest: A Christian Approach to the Priesthood of Christ*, Oxford: Oxford University Press, 2010, p. 90.
13 Pope John Paul II, *Ecclesia de Eucharistia*, 3.
14 Ibid., 12.

15 St John Chrysostom, *Homilies on Hebrews* 17.6, in O'Collins and Jones, *Jesus Our Priest*, p. 83.

16 *The Family Haggadah*, New York: Mesorah Publications, 1981, p. 27.

17 Pope John Paul II, *Ecclesia de Eucharistia*, 15.

18 Pope John Paul II, *Mane Nobiscum Domine*, 2004, 11.

19 Ibid., 11.

20 Ibid., 14.

21 Pope St Leo the Great, Sermon 1 on the Ascension, in *The Divine Office* II, Eastertide Week 6, London: Collins, 1974, p. 614. Emphasis added.

22 Pope Benedict XVI, *Sacramentum Caritatis*, 64.

23 Vatican II, *Gaudium et Spes*, 1965, 22.

24 *Sacrosanctum Concilium*, 47. See also *CCC*, 1382, and Pope John Paul II, *Ecclesia de Eucharistia*, 12. Emphasis added.

25 St John Chrysostom, Homily 50, 3–4, in *The Divine Office* III, Week 21, Saturday, London: Collins, 1974, pp. 480–1.

26 Pope Benedict XVI, Address to the Roman Curia, 22 December 2005, quoted in *Sacramentum Caritatis*, 66. Emphasis added.

27 Pope Benedict XVI, *Sacramentum Caritatis*, 31.

28 Henri de Lubac, 'Causes internes de l'atténuation et de la disparition du sens du Sacré', in *Bulletin des aumôniers catholiques. Chantiers de la jeunesse*, No. 31, (1942), republished in *Theology in History*, San Francisco: Ignatius Press, 1996, p. 230.

29 The mutual indwelling of the Persons of the Trinity was expressed by St John of Damascus (c.655–c.750) by the term *perichoresis*, though the idea was implicit in the Trinitarian theology of the Cappadocian Fathers and in Dionysius the Pseudo-Areopagite. Its rendition in Latin as *circumincessio* is attributed to Burgundio of Pisa (c.1110–c.1193).

30 Henri de Lubac, *The Splendor of the Church*, San Francisco: Ignatius Press, 1986, 1989, p. 237.

31 Aquinas, *Summa Theologiae*, IIIa, q. 62, a. 1, ad primum.

32 Pope Benedict XVI, *Sacramentum Caritatis*, 15.

33 *Sacrosanctum Concilium*, 14.

34 Pope Francis, *Desiderio Desideravi*, 2022, 36.

35 I am relying here on a conference paper given by Cardinal Kasper: 'Le diacre dans une perspective ecclésiologique face aux défis actuels de l'Eglise et de la société'.

36 Pope John Paul II, *Ecclesia de Eucharistia*, 22.

37 Joseph Ratzinger, 'Eucharist and Mission', *Irish Theological Quarterly*, Vol. 65 (2000), p. 263.

CHAPTER FIVE

SACRAMENTS OF HEALING AND WHOLENESS

INTRODUCTION

In this chapter we take account of the brokenness of humanity. Physical, mental and emotional illnesses cause pain and anguish to all people at some time in their lives. For some, this is a lifelong agony: mental or physical disability, paralysis, addiction, rejection and exposure to evil in its many guises, especially in abusive relationships. The sacraments respond to the suffering of humanity. Christ has personally experienced the pain of being human, to the point of enduring the death of a common criminal. To evoke the synodal image, he journeys with us, as he did with the two disciples on the road to Emmaus (Lk 24). He does so all the time, but this is made explicit in the different sacraments.

When adults are baptised they come in from the cold to be part of the community we call 'Church', the Church being the sacrament of Christ. In confirmation the Holy Spirit comes to replace fear and isolation with courage and a missionary spirit. In the Eucharist we are nourished in a tangible way: Jesus says, 'I am the bread of life. Whoever comes to me will never be hungry, and whoever believes in me will never be thirsty' (Jn 6:35). But it is in the sacraments of penance and the anointing of the sick that the healing power of Christ is especially manifest. We will reflect first of all on the sacrament of penance.

NAMING THE SACRAMENT

What has commonly been referred to as 'Confession' is more properly called the 'sacrament of penance', though it also bears the title 'sacrament of reconciliation'. Confession, penance and reconciliation are all aspects of the sacrament: we confess our sins, we undertake a penance to underline our seriousness about changing and we are reconciled with God and the Church. My preference is to refer to the sacrament as the 'sacrament of penance' because that is what was decided at the Council of Florence in 1439: 'The fourth sacrament is penance …'.[1]

A SACRAMENT IN CRISIS

There is little doubt but that the sacrament of penance is in crisis. It is frequented less and less by people in the average parish. Long gone are the days of the queues awaiting 'confession'. One can proffer several possible reasons for this. We will examine three issues here: the lack of the sense of sin; the misunderstanding of the concept of 'sacrament'; and rabid individualism.

Lack of the Sense of Sin

The lack of a sense of sin is surely one factor as to why this sacrament is in crisis. It is one of the consequences of the secular age. It is a grace to be aware of one's sinfulness and the need for God's forgiveness. I expect that Pope Francis gave us all pause for thought when, in his first papal interview in 2013, he was asked, 'Who is Jorge Borgolio?' He humbly answered: 'I am a sinner. This is the most accurate definition. It is not a figure of speech, a literary genre. I am a sinner.'[2] That answer does not indicate a negative anthropology but a realism on which a true humanity can be built. A key ingredient of this foundation is humility. Humility derives from the Latin word for ground, *humus*: it implies having one's feet on the ground. Humility is the mark of a true and authentic existence. Humility is often feigned and merely the mask covering puffed-up pride. It is only through our contemplation of Christ crucified that we can come to a true estimate of ourselves, and this includes a sense of sin and a need for God. True humility is built on the rock of truth; false humility is built on the shifting sands of a selfish ego (image from Mt 7:24-27). In a document published in 2015 to coincide with the Jubilee of Mercy, the Congregation for Divine Worship underlined the value and essential nature of humbly acknowledging our sinfulness:

> Recognising and repenting of one's sins is not a humiliation. Rather, it is a recovery of the true face of God and an abandonment of self with confidence to his loving plan while at the same time rediscovering our true human face, created in the image and likeness of God.[3]

There are three gems in this quotation. First, with humble repentance we recover the true face of God; second, we can entrust ourselves to God with confidence; and third, humble repentance enables us to discover our true selves. Again, this is not humiliation, because we find that our true selves are created in God's image and likeness.

Misunderstanding Sacraments

There are many other reasons why the sacrament of penance is less frequented nowadays. A faulty understanding of sacraments in general has seriously undermined this sacrament. All too often in the past the sacrament of penance was presented in a juridical way that led in some cases to serious scrupulosity (obsessive concern or anxiety over one's own sinfulness). The mercy of God was not uppermost; indeed it was sometimes hard to find. It is no wonder that the Vatican II document of the liturgy, *Sacrosanctum Concilium*, called for a renewal of this sacrament: 'The rite and formulae of Penance are to be revised so that they more clearly express both the nature and effect of the sacrament.'[4] We will see in the course of this chapter the extent to which this has been achieved. Of course, there are vast differences in its success rate in different countries.

Rabid Individualism

The question 'why confess to a priest?' is pertinent: why not confess directly to God? This issue is all the more pressing in a culture of rabid individualism. God can certainly forgive sin apart from the sacrament of penance. It is not God who needs the sacrament: it is a human need. We need the tangible, external experience that the sacrament offers.

Sometimes this is a cathartic experience; on other occasions it offers the reassurance we need of being reconciled to God and the Church. The *Catechism of the Catholic Church* states: 'Reconciliation with the Church is inseparable from reconciliation with God' (*CCC*, 1445). In devotional confessions – where the sin or sins are not serious – we are gifted with the grace of courage and strength for life's journey. The priest is present in the person of Christ the Head (*in persona Christi capitis*) and in the person of the Church (*in persona ecclesiae*). It is Christ who forgives and reconciles. The priest unfolds the richness of the sacrament as he invokes the Holy Spirit at the beginning and reads a brief extract from scripture. It is he who suggests a penance appropriate for the penitent. This may take the form of a charitable act and/or a prayer. He may also offer advice and guidance during the sacrament. The formula of absolution is rich in theology and compassion. It is Trinitarian; it draws its power from the death and resurrection of Christ; it acknowledges that this is an exercise of the Church for a particular person:

> God, the Father of mercies, through the death and resurrection of his Son has reconciled the world to himself and sent the Holy Spirit among us for the forgiveness of sins; through the ministry of the Church may God give you pardon and peace, and I absolve you from your sins in the name of the Father, and of the Son, and of the Holy Spirit.[5]

The holistic experience of reconciliation offered by the sacrament of penance, leading to 'pardon and peace', could not be achieved by a person on their own. It is not the case that the forgiving God is absent apart from the sacrament but that we need the relational and ritual experience the sacrament offers to be able to receive God's love and mercy.

Here we have arrived at the heart of the reason for sacraments. They are the tangible, existential presence of Christ and his Church. Without the sacraments our experience of God and his mercy could easily evaporate or become merely cerebral. In our first chapter we examined the anthropological underpinning of sacraments. Here we are seeing it in practice. The contemporaries of Jesus were brought to him that he might touch them and they were healed and forgiven. In John 9:1-8, we saw Jesus perform an elaborate ritual by which he healed the man born blind. Others were cured by merely touching the hem of his cloak. Bartimaeus was healed without a ritual: there was no physical contact between him and Jesus (Mk 10:46-52).

INSTITUTION BY CHRIST

On the day of resurrection Jesus appears to the disciples, who had locked themselves in a house for fear of the Jews. Jesus appears to them, breathes on them and speaks these words: 'Receive the Holy Spirit. If you forgive the sins of any, they are forgiven them; if you retain the sins of any, they are retained' (Jn 20:22-23). Breath is always associated with impartation of the Holy Spirit. In the older of the two accounts of creation in Genesis, God breathes into the nostrils of man 'the breath of life; and the man became a living being' (Gn 2:7). In the Johannine Pentecost, God enables the apostles to bring about a new creation through the forgiveness of sin. Jesus transfers the power of forgiveness to his fledgling Church. St Augustine has this to say about the event: 'For it is not only Peter but the whole Church which binds and looses sins.'[6] This power is handed down through apostolic succession. When given the faculty to do so by their bishop, priests exercise the power given on the day of the Lord's resurrection. The *Catechism of the Catholic Church* gives a cogent summary of the function of the priest in the sacrament of penance, drawing on some of the parables of Jesus that show God's mercy:

> When he celebrates the sacrament of Penance, the priest is fulfilling the ministry of the Good Shepherd who seeks the lost sheep, of the Good Samaritan who binds up wounds, of the Father who awaits the prodigal son and welcomes him on his return … The priest is the sign and the instrument of God's merciful love for the sinner. (*CCC*, 1465)

GUILT SHEDDING OR TRUE CONVERSION

Jesus began his preaching with a call to repentance: 'The time is fulfilled, and the kingdom of God has come near; repent, and believe in the good news' (Mk 1:15; see also Mt 4:17). But we do not repent by our own power. St Paul makes this clear in his letters: 'In Christ God was reconciling the world to himself' (2 Cor 5:19). Christ died so that we might be reconciled: 'For if while we were enemies, we were reconciled to God through the death of his Son, much more surely, having been reconciled, will we be saved by his life' (Rm 5:10).

The Council of Trent listed three acts of repentance on the part of the penitent: contrition, confession and satisfaction (or penance). The rite of penance (*Ordo Paenitentiae*, 1974) reiterates these elements of the sacrament, highlighting contrition as the most important. Contrition means an inner conversion of the heart (*metanoia*):

> We can only approach the Kingdom of Christ by *metanoia*. This is a profound change of the whole person by which one begins to consider, judge, and arrange one's life according to the holiness and love of God.[7]

Conversion takes place at the level of the heart, that is, in the depths of our being (*CCC*, 368). This is a far cry from a juridical approach to the sacrament. Moreover, it should not be a way of just off-loading guilt. For that reason one must prepare for the sacrament beforehand with an honest examination of conscience. We can only achieve that with the aid of the Holy Spirit, who gives us the courage to face our true selves and confess our sins honestly and humbly. It is well-nigh impossible to do this outside of the sacramental context. When we know we will be in dialogue with a priest, we can clarify our sins for ourselves and prepare to articulate them.

I do not mean to belittle the fact that guilt is lifted in the sacrament of penance. Being freed from guilt can open the way to a new beginning, a fresh start. However, seeing the sacrament as just a means of guilt-shedding is dangerous: it can leave the root causes of our sin untouched and we may slip again all too easily. I believe that the sacrament has been used by some criminals to allay the promptings of conscience and to return to their nefarious ways. This is why it is important to prioritise conversion when we prepare for the sacrament.

THE FIVE WAYS OF REPENTANCE

St John Chrysostom proposed five ways of repentance.[8] First of all, we need to acknowledge our sins. He calls this 'the royal road to repentance'. The second, we need to forgive others: 'Forgive us our trespasses as we forgive those who trespass against us,' as Jesus taught us to say in the Our Father. The third way of repentance is prayer: 'fervent and diligent prayer, prayer from the heart'. The fourth is almsgiving, meaning giving of oneself to others in charity. The fifth and final way highlighted by St John Chrysostom is humility: 'Modest and humble behaviour … annihilates sin as drastically as the other methods. The Publican bears witness to this. He had no good deeds but instead he offered humility and the burden of his sins dropped off him.' An anonymous second-century author has this to say about almsgiving: 'Almsgiving is one form of repentance and a good one too; fasting is better than prayer; but almsgiving is better than both, because charity covers a multitude of sins.'[9] The *Catechism of the Catholic Church* draws attention to the fact that scripture and the Fathers insist on prayer, fasting and almsgiving 'which express conversion in relation to oneself, to God, and to others' (*CCC*, 1434).

FORMS OF THE SACRAMENT OF PENANCE

The norm for the celebration of the sacrament of penance today is the meeting between priest and penitent in the privacy of the confessional. This was not the case in the early centuries of the Church. At that time the sacrament was possible only once and, as a result, was postponed as long as possible, even to the end of one's life. Three sins, in particular, were regarded as especially heinous: apostasy, homicide and adultery. Sinners were obliged to perform public penances as an expression of their repentance. These penances involved sitting in sackcloth and ashes in the public square. The practice of private confession and penance was introduced in the sixth century by Irish monks. Since Vatican II there is the option of communal celebrations of the sacrament, though this must include the individual confession of sins and individual absolution. Parishes offer this option during Advent and Lent or on some special occasions, such as a pilgrimage or retreat. This form has the advantage of highlighting that sin and repentance have community dimensions. There is also a third option, a communal celebration of the sacrament with general absolution, on the occasion of grave necessity (*CCC*, 1483). By that is meant that individual confession is not possible because of the danger of death or the lack of priests to administer the sacrament in a reasonable time. It is the responsibility of the local ordinary (i.e., the bishop) to determine if the conditions necessary for this third form are present (*Code of Canon Law* [*CIC*], 961). A priest is obliged to consult his ordinary before celebrating this form of the sacrament. If he is unable to do so, he must inform his bishop as soon as is possible after the event. One thinks of a war situation where people are unable to receive the sacrament in the usual way and where the priest has no means of consulting the bishop, such as in the bunkers in Ukraine where hundreds of people were in immediate danger of death. Another instance was presented by the Covid-19 crisis. At the beginning of the pandemic the Holy See issued a document on the matter. It emphasised that individual confession and absolution remained the norm but that certain circumstances may arise whereby a priest could give general absolution, for example at the entrance to a hospital ward where people were in danger of death. This document also emphasised that sins can be forgiven apart from the sacrament by a sincere act of repentance:

> Where the individual faithful find themselves in the painful impossibility of receiving sacramental absolution, it should be remembered that perfect contrition, coming from the love of God, beloved above all things, expressed by a sincere request for forgiveness (that which the penitent is at present able to express) and accompanied by *votum confessionis*, that is, by the firm resolution to have recourse, as soon as possible, to sacramental confession, obtains forgiveness of sins, even mortal ones (cf. *CCC*, no. 1452).[10]

Pope Francis drew attention to this truth in March 2020, giving assurance that sins can be forgiven by sincerely turning to God. This is not new. St Thomas Aquinas taught that sins can be forgiven if we sincerely repent and are awaiting the sacrament. Again, it must be stressed that we need to have the resolve to seek out the sacrament at the earliest opportunity.

In his post-synodal apostolic exhortation *Reconciliatio et Paenitentia* (1984), Pope John Paul II highlighted the faithful's obligation to follow the norms 'including that of not having recourse again to general absolution before a normal integral and individual confession of sins, which must be made as soon as possible'.[11] He asked priests to inform and instruct the faithful about this norm in particular before granting absolution.

The *Catechism of the Catholic Church* distinguishes between mortal and venial sin. Mortal sin destroys charity in the heart of a person, while venial sin offends and wounds charity but does not destroy it (*CCC*, 1855). It can be helpful to distinguish three categories of sin: mortal, grave and venial sin. Mortal sin is a state of sinfulness that comes about as a result of a constant turning away from God. Three conditions are necessary before we can nominate a sin as mortal. These are: grievous matter, full knowledge and full consent (*CCC*, 1857). Grave sins are particular acts or omissions that can best be illustrated in terms of the Ten Commandments. Venial sins are less serious offences against God and neighbour where the three conditions mentioned above are not present.

GOD'S MERCY

The key to the sacrament of penance is mercy – God's mercy. It is important to emphasise that it is God's mercy, not the limited mercy of which humans are capable, often based on mere tolerance with little concern for the seriousness of sin. Luke's gospel is the gospel of mercy: 'Be merciful, just as your Father is merciful' (Lk 6:36). Matthew, on the other hand, highlights perfection: 'Be perfect, therefore, as your heavenly Father is perfect' (Mt 5:48). There are two parables, unique to St Luke, that illustrate God's mercy and Jesus' discernment of sin: the Prodigal Son (Lk 15:11-32) and the Pharisee and the Publican (Lk 18:9-14). In the first parable we have two sinners, the tearaway younger son and his self-righteous elder brother. The younger son repents and returns home, humbly confessing his sins: he meets with unconditional love and mercy. The elder son shows lack of forgiveness to his brother and laments that his own faithful service has not been rewarded. He manifests a paralysing pride. He corresponds very much to the Pharisee in the second parable. The Pharisee has an inflated sense of his own self-importance. In contrast, the Publican is aware of his sinfulness and humbly confesses: 'God, be merciful to me, a sinner!' Jesus tells us that this sinner went home at rights with God while the other did not. Jesus is clear that recognition of one's sins, despite their gravity, and humble contrition provide the fertile ground on which God can lavish his mercy.

THE SACRAMENT OF THE SICK

Closely connected with the sacrament of penance is the sacrament of the sick. Both sacraments have their roots in scripture: the words and actions of Jesus are foundational to these sacraments. He healed the sick and forgave sins. The Twelve followed suit: 'They cast out many demons, and anointed with oil many who were sick and cured them' (Mk 6:13).

This practice continued, as is evidenced by this advice in the Letter of St James:

> Are any among you sick? They should call for the elders of the church and have them pray over them, anointing them with oil in the name of the Lord. The prayer of faith will save the sick, and the Lord will raise them up; and anyone who has committed sins will be forgiven. (Jas 5:14-15)

The essentials of the sacrament of the sick as we celebrate it today are to be found in this quotation. The elders are the priests (*presbuteroi*), prayer 'over' the sick person implies the invocation of the Holy Spirit (*epiclesis*) and the anointing with oil is also symbolic of the Holy Spirit. One aspect of the sacrament that is rarely emphasised is the forgiveness of sins. The sacrament of the sick aims to heal body, mind and spirit. The term 'elders' does not mean older people but those who have authority in the Church.

Naming the Sacrament

Traditionally, the sacrament was called 'extreme unction', or the anointing of the dying. The Second Vatican Council advised a less rigorous use of the sacrament and renamed it the 'anointing of the sick'.[12] It would henceforth be offered to people who were seriously ill, though not necessarily on the point of death. It is also administered to people facing serious surgery.

Celebrating the Sacrament

The ceremony begins with a sprinkling of holy water, which recalls baptism. Following a brief introduction, a penitential rite is carried out for the sick person and those present. An important part of this, and all sacraments, is the proclamation of the Word of God. As Karl Rahner has rightly said, no sacrament should be celebrated without some reading from scripture. The priest may deliver a brief homily and relate the reading (or readings) to the actual situation. This leads to the rite itself, which begins with a prayer over the oil that has been blessed by the bishop at the Chrism Mass on Holy Thursday. Alternatively, if that is not available, a prayer of blessing is given in the ritual (*CCC*, 1519). The priest may impose hands on the sick person's head to evoke the presence of the Holy Spirit (*epiclesis*). At this stage the anointing of the forehead and hands takes place. Previously, all the senses were anointed via the mouth, nose, ears, eyes, hands and feet. With the revised rite the anointing is confined to hands and forehead.

The accompanying prayers are deeply evocative. When anointing the forehead, the priest says, 'Through this holy anointing may the Lord in his love and mercy help you with the grace of the Holy Spirit.' Then he anoints the hands, saying, 'May the Lord who frees you from sin save you and raise you up.' These prayers clearly indicate that the sacrament of the sick is not necessarily for physical healing. Its primary purpose is to give spiritual strength, which comes from the Holy Spirit. The prayer over the hands makes explicit two key scriptural terms: salvation and resurrection. The sacrament of the sick contributes to the salvation of the sick and, ultimately, to their participation in the resurrection of Christ. There is a concluding prayer that takes account of the existential situation: terminal illness, advanced age, before surgery, for a child or for a young person. The ceremony ends with the Our Father.

The sacrament may also be celebrated during Mass. In fact, the *Catechism* suggests that this is the more fitting context for the sacrament of the sick (*CCC*, 1517). If circumstances allow, the sacrament of penance may be celebrated before the Mass. Even apart from Mass, Communion may be given. In this context it is called *Viaticum*, meaning that it is food for the journey (*via*).

It may not always be possible to celebrate the full rite. Sometimes there may not be enough time, such as when the person is on the point of death. In a hospital situation the medical team may be busily attempting to save the person's life, for example following an accident. In that case the priest may only be able to anoint one part of the body and recite the prayers quietly in the background: 'In case of necessity, however, it is sufficient that a single anointing be given on the forehead or, because of the particular condition of the sick person, on another more suitable part of the body, the whole formula being pronounced.'[13]

Notes

1   Heinrich Denzinger, *Enchiridion Symbolorum: Compendium of Creeds, Definitions, and Declarations on Matters of Faith and Morals*, 43rd edn, ed. Peter Hünermann, Robert Fastiggi and Anne Englund Nash, San Francisco: Ignatius Press, 2012, 1323.

2   Pope Francis, interview with Antonio Spadaro, 'A Big Heart Open to God: An Interview with Pope Francis', *America*, Vol. 209, No. 8 (30 September 2013).

3   Congregation for Divine Worship and the Discipline of the Sacraments, *Rediscovering the Rite of Penance*, 2015, Introduction.

4   Vatican II, *Sacrosanctum Concilium*, 1963, 72.

5   Pope Paul VI, *Ordo Paenitentiae*, 1974, 46.

6   St Augustine, Homily 124, *The Divine Office* II, London: Collins, 1974, p. 650.

7   Pope Paul VI, *Paenitemini*, 1966.

8   St John Chrysostom, 'On the Devil' 2, 6, *The Divine Office* III, London: Collins, 1974, pp. 464–5.

9   Homily of a second-century author, *The Divine Office* III, p. 755.

10 Apostolic Penitentiary, *Note from the Apostolic Penitentiary on the Sacrament of Reconciliation in the Current Pandemic*, 20 March 2020.

11 Pope John Paul II, *Reconciliatio et Paenitentia*, 1984, 33.

12 *Sacrosanctum Concilium*, 73.

13 Pope Paul VI, *Sacram Unctione Infirmorum*, 1972.

CHAPTER SIX

THE SACRAMENT OF MARRIAGE: SECULAR REALITY AND SAVING MYSTERY

INTRODUCTION

There is such a variety of places nowadays where a couple can be married: a plush hotel, an exotic castle or a beach in a faraway place. So, when a couple decides to get married in a church it is no longer the inevitable location; it is a free choice. What happens in the church, however, is that they receive a new sacrament. But marriage existed long before it became a sacrament, so we will need to explore the history of marriage, beginning with pre-Christian marriage, and the idea of marriage as sacrament.

Marriage has its origin in creation: 'Marriage as such belongs to the creatural order, within the divine plan.'[1] This is expressed in the first book of the bible: 'So God created humankind in his image, in the image of God he created them; male and female he created them' (Gn 1:27). As Walter Kasper points out, 'The sexual difference clearly forms an essential part of humanity's created being.'[2] All societies have had to discover how best to incorporate this fact of creation into their social, economic, political and religious institutions.

Marriage, then, is primarily a gift of human nature. God made man and woman to find fulfilment and completion in one another. Marriage wasn't invented by the Church; it is part of creation from the beginning: 'God himself is the author of marriage'.[3] The bride and groom are ministers of the sacrament of marriage to each other. The priest doesn't marry them. He is there as a witness on behalf of the Church and he blesses the union. His role underlines the fact that marriage is an ecclesial event. We will examine the mixed views and debates around this question and the differing conclusions arrived at by the Eastern and Western Churches.

Jesus raised marriage to the level of a sacrament. This means that the marriage of two baptised people is a living sign of God's love relationship with humanity. It is of no small significance that when God wanted a human sign of his own enormous love for us that he chose the marriage relationship. The dominant image of God's relationship with humanity in the Old Testament is the nuptial one: humanity is God's spouse. There are several instances where the spouse is unfaithful to God, but God's love remains undiminished. As the Song of Songs exclaims: 'Love is strong as death, passion fierce as the grave … Many waters cannot quench love' (Song 8:6-7). Marriage is a sign of this love.

But to say that a married couple is a sign of God's love in the world is not the full story. It is a sign with a difference. The difference is that God's love is present in every marriage. God is the third party in the marriage relationship. God is present in the sign. That is such good news for every married couple and for those who believe their Christian vocation is marriage. Like any gift, the gift that is the sacrament of marriage needs to be unwrapped and used. A sacrament is not a magical event; it doesn't work automatically. It needs human receptivity and cooperation.

The sacramental understanding of marriage developed gradually over several centuries, though it had its roots in scripture. The Church gives prime importance to the presence of Jesus at the wedding in Cana (Jn 2:1-11): 'She sees in it the confirmation of the goodness of marriage and the proclamation that henceforth marriage will be an efficacious sign of Christ's presence' (*CCC*, 1613). Jesus stressed the permanence of marriage with God as its author: 'What God has joined together, let no one separate' (Mt 19:6 and Mk 10:9).

Up until the eleventh century, marriage among Christians was seen as a secular reality to be experienced 'in the Lord' and deserving of pastoral care in the moral and religious sense. It was in the period from the eleventh century to the middle of the thirteenth century that it came to be understood theologically as a sacrament. This understanding was arrived at through a long and arduous process. The full blossoming of the theology of marriage as sacrament is to be found in the writings of St Thomas Aquinas, namely the *Summa Theologiae* and the *Summa Contra Gentiles*.

PRE-CHRISTIAN MARRIAGE

We will begin with an exploration of the rites of marriage in pre-Christian times. Greek and Roman customs surrounding marriage were similar in many respects. In both cultures the solemnisation of marriage was a sacral act but it was not based on personal relationships or even on procreation. Roman religion in the seventh century BCE was a religion of the hearth, the fire being the symbol of the household gods. The Roman household gods were *manes*, *lares* and *penates*. Each family had its own household liturgy that was particular to that family and no other. The role of the priest was performed by the father, known as the *paterfamilias*, and this function was passed from father to son.

When a woman got married she moved from one religion (or family) to another. There were three stages in a wedding. First was the *traditio puellae*, the handing over of the bride, which took place in her father's house. Second, the *domum-ductio* or the solemn taking of the bride to the bridegroom's house. The bride wore a veil and a garland and was seated in a carriage as the procession moved from her father's house to her new home (and religion). The *confarreatio* (Greek: *telos*) was the final ceremony, and it took place in the bridegroom's house. The bride was taken over the threshold of the house by the bridegroom and brought to the 'altar', which was the fire or hearth. There was a wedding cake, of which both partook. But it was through communion with the household gods that they entered communion with one another. The bridegroom had the authority of *paterfamilias*. Marriage was therefore a religious act whereby a woman was initiated into a different religion. At a later stage the wedding ceremony was divided between the home and the temple, thus taking on a more public dimension.

101

The birth of a child was followed nine or ten days later by a religious act in the family, which we may interpret as a ceremony of initiation. Though the emphasis for continuity's sake was on the father–son relationship, the wife enjoyed equal dignity with her husband. Women were far more emancipated in the Greco-Roman world than, for example, in the Semitic society.

From the seventh to the fifth centuries BCE, Greek and Roman society became more secular, with a corresponding weakening of the religious understanding of marriage. The new secular marriage was based on the mutual consent of husband and wife. The wife-to-be would live with her future husband for a year (the *usus*) before the marriage, which was now a purely secular affair with no religious ceremony. In imperial times, coinciding with the Christian era, a marriage was effected by the mutual consent of the parties alone, with no other formalities such as the *usus*.

CHRISTIAN MARRIAGE IN THE EARLY CHURCH

As late as the Council of Elvira (*c*.300 or 310), Christian marriages were celebrated in a way similar to pagan marriages. Admittedly, Ignatius of Antioch (*c*.50–*c*.117), in his letter to Polycarp (69–155), stressed the connection between the bishop and the marriage of Christians: 'And it is proper for men and women who marry to be united with the consent of the bishop, that the marriage may be in accordance with the Lord and not due to lustful passions.'[4] This would seem to imply a strong Christian – perhaps liturgical – aspect to marriage. But this was not the case. The admonition of St Ignatius seems to have been a lone voice at that time and was not put into practice. Marriage at this time was regarded as a secular reality. What was important for Christians was that they married 'in the Lord', a phrase which goes back to St Paul (1 Cor 7:39). The meaning of this term 'in the Lord' was very precise in the early centuries of the Church. It meant that a Christian could only marry a Christian, though the marriage took place according to the prevailing secular culture.

In the fourth century we find evidence of the blessing of a marriage by a bishop or a priest who happened to visit the family on the occasion of the wedding. Gradually this developed into a liturgy. But the liturgy of marriage was an adjunct to the 'real' marriage, which was still a civil contract within the family circle. No Church law governed marriage in this period. So a 'Church marriage' was very different from our understanding of the term; it was a marriage between two baptised Christians that took the form of a secular rite. If a Mass was celebrated, it confirmed the marriage but was not integral to the marriage itself, though the Christian virtues and the grace of the Mass were emphasised as important for the couple. The fourth and fifth centuries, then, are regarded as the period when the nuptial Mass followed the civil marriage contract in the Roman (Western) Church. This Mass included the priestly solemnisation of the marriage. However, there was no obligation to have a nuptial Mass or to have the priestly solemnisation. This situation continued throughout the first millennium. The Church accepted in practice the legislative and judicial power of the state in matrimonial matters, including those affecting Christians. The obligation to have a liturgical marriage ceremony dates from the eleventh century, but this was only formalised and defined at the Council of Trent.

SCHOLASTIC PERIOD

Edward Schillebeeckx is of the view that, from the eleventh to the thirteenth centuries, marriage was regarded as a sacrament not because of the liturgy surrounding it but, rather, 'because of the nature of the event of marriage itself'.[5] The latter phrase means that in the early part of the second millennium there was an exceptionally strong sense of marriage as emanating from creation, with God as its author. But it was not yet seen as a sacrament as we understand it. If we turn to the Fathers of the Church we don't find a strong sense of marriage as sacrament. A distrust of sexuality didn't augur well for a theology of the marital sacrament. The Church Fathers tended to emphasise the moral and religious demands of Christian married life and did not comment in detail on the significance of the rite of marriage itself. Their interpretation of Ephesians 5:21-32 did not elicit from the text the understanding of marriage that we readily find in it today. Like St Paul, they saw it as a text that highlights an understanding of the Church as the bride of Christ. Though St Augustine called marriage a *'sacramentum'* on the basis of the Ephesians text, it would be an overstretched reading that would conclude that Augustine understood marriage as a sacrament in the sense in which that term was used in the thirteenth century. But he did see marriage as a sacred sign of the unity between Christ and his Church. This understanding pertained for several centuries.

An extended debate occurred in the Middle Ages as to what constituted a marriage. This is more a canonical question, but it is important to mention it here. There were two schools of thought, which we can loosely nominate as the *consensus* school and the *copula* school. The first was of the view that the consent of the parties was all that was necessary for a marriage (as supported by Isidore of Seville [560–636]). The copula view was that consent alone was not sufficient; the marriage had to be consummated (*ratum et consummatum*) to qualify as a marriage (supported by Hincmar of Rheims [806–82] and the Frankish Church). The Fathers of the Church, especially Augustine, believed that marriage was possible even without sexual intercourse. Hugh of St Victor, so important in the development of the theology of sacraments in the twelfth century, based his treatise on marriage on the consensus theory. The canonists, on the other hand, favoured the copula theory. Gratian (the twelfth-century jurist) brought the two theories together in this way: a marriage by consensus, though valid, was dissoluble; a consummated marriage was indissoluble.

BLESSING OR VEILING

I have already mentioned the custom that developed quite early on whereby a bishop or priest was invited to give a blessing following a marriage ceremony, a ceremony that, at the time, was purely secular. The custom of veiling the couple, as a symbol of the blessing, grew between the fifth and tenth centuries. By the eleventh century the blessing of the couple was reduced to the blessing of the bride. Following St Paul's teaching in 1 Corinthians 11:2-15, it was believed that the man, being in the image of God (v. 7), did not need to be veiled. The woman, on the other hand, being a reflection of man (also v. 7), needed to be blessed, with the blessing symbolised by the veil.

Some commentators presume that the veiling of the bride has its origin in pre-Christian Roman times, but this is not the case. The veiling has more to do with the tradition of veiling the virgin on the occasion of her consecration. Prior to Vatican II, religious sisters and nuns wore the full bridal gown and veil on the occasion of their reception into religious life. The veiling in the sacrament of marriage owes more to the consecration of virginity for the sake of the kingdom of God than it does to ancient Roman and Greek rites. We can establish, then, a correlation between esteem for the consecrated life and appreciation of marriage. Celibacy and marriage both witness to kingdom values but do so differently. The consecrated virgin or celibate is an eschatological sign of the kingdom, while marriage, as a secular reality, is an experience of the kingdom here and now (the already but not yet).

MANICHEAN INFLUENCES

Manichaeism (after Mani, 216–274) spread negative attitudes to sexuality and marriage. It taught that the material world was evil and thus so was marriage. In the twelfth century its influence was strong through sects like the Catharists and the Albigensians, both of which were condemned at the Second Lateran Council in 1139. As a result, theologians were obliged to present the sacred character of marriage with urgency. This historical crisis led to the definition of marriage as sacrament, with due emphasis on the goodness and holiness of marriage. From this developed two distinct theories.

One theory proposed that it is the priest's solemnisation or blessing that makes marriage a sacrament. St Bonaventure (*c.*1217–74) and St Albert the Great (1200–80) were of this view. This was also the view in the Eastern Church, a view that pertains to this day. In other words, the Orthodox churches of the East regard the priest as the one who effects the sacrament of marriage. This means that in the Eastern Church the liturgical celebration is the real sacrament of marriage.

The second proposal was that marriage is a sacrament by virtue of the *consensus* of the partners. In other words, it is the couple who bring about the sacrament. Hugh of St Victor took this view. Duns Scotus (1266–1308) was more explicit still: the sacrament is not administered by the priest but by the bride and bridegroom together. The Western Church continues this tradition.

The obligation to have the marriage celebrated in a liturgical setting dates from the Council of Trent in the sixteenth century. The Council solemnly declared that marriage was one of the seven sacraments.[6] Following Trent, the only valid marriage for two baptised Christians was one that took place in the presence of a priest (typically the parish priest or a priest delegated by him) and two witnesses.[7] The ecclesial legal form of marriage dates from Trent, however, the Council also recognised the jurisdictional powers of the state in regard to marriage.

SEPTENARIUM

In the scholastic period (twelfth and thirteenth centuries), a *sacramentum* was seen as an effective symbol, not just a representative symbol. By 'effective' was meant that some change was brought about. In Rahnerian terms, we might say that marriage as sacrament moved from being a 'representative' symbol (of the unity between Christ and his Church) to being a 'real' symbol of that unity. For the Fathers of the Church, the dissolution of marriage was not permissible; for the scholastics, dissolution was not possible. The latter position was attributable to the efficacy of the sacrament (efficient causality).

In the twelfth century marriage began to be understood as a sacrament in the full meaning of *sacramentum*, that is, as an effective sign of grace. Up until then marriage was seen as a *sacramentum-signum*, i.e. a sign of the mystery of Christ and his Church. That understanding went back to Augustine. What is particularly interesting is that the consecration of virgins and the anointing of kings were regarded as being effective signs of grace, but neither was included in the *septenarium* (the seven sacraments precisely defined).[8] Marriage was part of the *septenarium* before it was defined as an effective sign of grace. When first it was included among the seven, marriage was not regarded as having a saving power (grace). Obviously, marriage was seen as most important for the Christian life, and for that reason it was part of the *septenarium* while the consecration of virgins was not. In this perspective, the life of faith preceded theology. Schillebeeckx expresses this idea as follows: 'Awareness in faith of the distinct sacramental meaning of marriage clearly preceded the theological expression of its sacramental significance.'[9] We may interpret this as an example of the exercise of the *sensus fidelium* (the sense of faith of the faithful).[10] The manner in which marriage came to be part of the seven sacraments is an example of how dogma develops: life and faith precede theology.

NEGATIVE ANTHROPOLOGY

A negative anthropology (a negative view of the body and all things human) made the acceptance of marriage as a means of grace difficult to accept for the scholastics. Two issues in particular caused this difficulty. First, the financial bartering that preceded a marriage was seen as incompatible with an understanding of marriage as a sacrament in the full sense. Second, the suspicion of sexuality, going back to the

Fathers, added to the scholastic reservations. The Fathers saw marriage as a *remedium concupiscentiae*, a 'remedy for concupiscence', i.e. a means of preventing sin. This view persisted into the twentieth century despite marriage being one of the seven sacraments. The Eastern Church did not have this negative view of sexuality.

Quite a lot of disagreement engaged the scholastics on the question of the source of grace in marriage. Some, such as William of Auvergne (1180–1249), attributed it to the priest's liturgical action; others, such as St Bonaventure, came to regard it as emanating from the *consensus* of the couple. St Bonaventure believed that marriage conferred grace on those who contracted it worthily. A full flowering of the sacramental nature of marriage can be found in the writings of St Albert the Great and St Thomas Aquinas. Their view was ratified at the Council of Trent.

THOMISTIC SUMMARY
St Thomas Aquinas recognised three aspects of marriage:

1. *Officium naturae*: Marriage as it devolves from nature. As a creature the human person is commissioned to perpetuate the species. Procreation and the raising of a family devolves from the *officium naturae*.

2. *Officium civilitatis*: Marriage as a civic duty, i.e. marriage as an anthropological and social phenomenon with civil, political and social responsibilities. This includes the mutual love of the partners. It has to do with the home and family life as well as civic society. The *officium civilitatis* is the human acting out of the *officium naturae*.

3. *Sacramentum*: In Aquinas' view Christ raised the *officium naturae* and the *officium civilitatis* to the level of a sacrament. To evoke the binary of matter and form, these *officia* were the matter of the sacrament of marriage. Its sacramental character did not diminish the secular reality of marriage but brought it under the ambit of Christian salvation. The secular reality, consisting of the *officium naturae* and the *officium civilitatis*, is now an effective instrument of God's grace. We should not be surprised to find that a secular reality becomes an instrument of grace because salvation comes to us in historical form.

Schillebeeckx summarises this important insight: 'An ordinary secular reality was seen to be an effective instrument of salvation in married and family life by virtue of Christ's redemption.'[11] This is the essence of our understanding of marriage as a sacrament.

It may be helpful to invoke the Chalcedonian Christological principle on the relationship between the two natures in Christ. They are 'without confusion, without change, without division, without separation'.[12] This means that raising marriage to the level of a sacrament does not make the secular reality of marriage otiose. For this reason I have given as title to this chapter 'Secular Reality and Saving Mystery'. Marriage doesn't cease to be a secular reality when it becomes a sacrament. The corollary is also true: the marriage of two baptised Christians is not just a natural marriage.

MARRIAGE BELONGS TO THE ORDER OF CREATION AND THE ORDER OF REDEMPTION[13]

While marriage is firstly a creaturely reality, it also has significant spiritual dimensions. This should not surprise us, because the human and the spiritual are not opposed to each other. As in Christ, the human and the divine coexist. All love comes from God, so married love is suffused with God who is love: 'Authentic married love is caught up into divine love and is directed and enriched by the redemptive power of Christ and the salvific action of the Church'.[14] The most fitting place for the celebration of marriage is the Mass 'because of the connection of all the sacraments with the Paschal mystery of Christ' (*CCC*, 1621). A sacramental marriage may be celebrated in a non-Catholic church ceremony, provided permission is received from the Catholic diocesan bishop. This is known as a dispensation from canonical form. The dispensation is essential for validity. Reception of the sacrament of penance is recommended to bride and groom as a preparation for the sacrament of marriage (*CCC*, 1622).

LICEITY AND VALIDITY

Given that a marriage comes about through the consent of the couple, it is important to clarify some issues surrounding the validity of the sacrament. First, the consent must be freely given. Where there is pressure to get married, the consent is most likely impaired and the marriage is invalid. Second, both bride and groom must intend their relationship to be permanent and exclusive: one is taking this person – and this person only – for the rest of one's life: 'The matrimonial union of man and woman is indissoluble' (*CCC*, 1614). Finally, the couple must be open to the possibility of having children. If this is excluded, then the marriage is invalid. In summary, then, marriage is a permanent sacrament between a man and a woman that entails indissolubility, fidelity and fruitfulness.

In the case of a marriage between a Catholic and a non-Catholic Christian (called a 'mixed marriage'), permission needs to be granted by the ecclesiastical authority. This is necessary for liceity (*CCC*, 1635; *CIC*, 1124). Marriage between a Catholic and a non-Christian presents an impediment to validity and requires a dispensation from the ecclesiastical authority. This is known as dispensation from 'disparity of cult' (*CCC*, 1635; *CIC*, 1086).

MARRIAGE PREPARATION

The preparation for marriage begins in the family. Growing up in a loving, faith-filled home can be described as privileged marriage preparation. Whatever pre-marriage course a couple does in advance of the wedding, while important, is unlikely to make up for an impoverished experience of marriage and family life. The parish community has a responsibility to signal the beauty and value of a loving marriage relationship. Walter Kasper captures this point when he writes: 'Perhaps the most important service that the Church has to carry out, however, is that of making young people capable of loving on the basis of Christian faith.'[15] The connection between love and faith needs to be central to our catechesis and teaching. If a young person grows up inspired by faith in Christ and in imitation of his self-giving, then such a person is in a good position to enter an exclusive relationship for life. The challenge faced by every couple is how to transform 'being in love' into a selfless, loving relationship. They take each other on their wedding day not just for better, for richer and in health but even, if not especially, when these are absent. This is unconditional love, which doesn't come easily to any human being. The power of the Holy Spirit can transform disappointment, negativity and disillusionment. This is the grace of the sacrament of marriage. It enables a couple to make the decision to love even if they don't feel like it. Some have described the love relationship as a movement from romance to disillusionment and again to joy, and this is a continuous process.

In the context of marriage and the Christian life generally, it is appropriate to recall the Greek distinction between four kinds of love. First, there is the love that is characteristic of family relationships, i.e. the love of parents for children and vice versa. This is called *storgé*. The second kind of love is friendship, *philia*. Love as passionate desire is *éros*. Finally, the love we find in the New Testament, *agapé*, is a total self-giving, as manifested by Christ on the cross.[16] The good Christian marriage and family will manifest all four types of love. This does not happen automatically, especially in contemporary secular society. Prayer is an important gift that helps open up the grace of the sacrament – family prayer and community prayer. A newly married couple have so much to offer their local parish and so much to gain from it. When children arrive they become part of the parish so naturally if their parents are already involved.

But the parish too has its responsibilities. The responsibility to ensure that people are prepared for marriage lies with the pastor of the parish under the direction of the bishop. The *Code of Canon Law* teases out four stages of this preparation: preaching and catechetics, preparation of the spouses for their impending wedding, fruitful celebration of the marriage liturgy and support for those who have entered marriage (*CIC*, 1063). Bishop Fintan Gavin has published a detailed analysis of the issues raised by canon 1063.[17] In addition to extensive scholarly resources, he examines the forms of preparation found in various countries, especially Spain and the United States. One readily concludes that marriage preparation in its four stages is a most urgent pastoral need. The different forms of preparation complement one another, for example continuous marriage enrichment is fertile terrain for remote marriage preparation.

CONCLUSION

It is important to point out that the sacraments themselves complement one another. The fruits of the Spirit highlighted in the sacrament of confirmation are the life blood of the Christian life and of marriage, in particular: 'love, joy, peace, patience, kindness, goodness, trustfulness, gentleness and self-control' (Gal 5:22-3). While marriage is obviously the way in which most people live out their baptism, this initial sacrament has another important dimension that is rarely appreciated. The family, which is known as the domestic Church, is an expression of the priesthood of the baptised 'in a privileged way' (*CCC*, 1657):

'In what might be regarded as the domestic Church, the parents, by word and example, are the first heralds of the faith with regard to their children.'[18] We will see in the next chapter the richness that is implied in the understanding of the priesthood of the baptised. It is, in fact, the basis of synodality.

Finally, the close relationship between marriage and the Eucharist has always been emphasised. It is expressed cogently by Pope Benedict XVI in his apostolic exhortation following the synod on the Eucharist:

> The Eucharist inexhaustibly strengthens the indissoluble unity and love of every Christian marriage. … The mutual consent that husband and wife exchange in Christ, which establishes them as a community of life and love, also has a eucharistic dimension. Indeed … conjugal love is a sacramental sign of Christ's love for his Church, a love culminating in the Cross, the origin and heart of the Eucharist.[19]

Given the intimate connection between these two sacraments, active participation by couples and families in Sunday Mass is the *sine qua non* of a happy marriage and family life.

Notes

1   International Theological Commission, *The Reciprocity Between Faith and Sacraments in the Sacramental Economy*, 2020, 135.

2   Walter Kasper, *Theology of Christian Marriage*, London: Burns & Oates, 1980, p. 26.

3   Vatican II, *Gaudium et Spes*, 1965, 48.

4   Ignatius, *Letter to Polycarp*, 5:1, in Michael W. Holmes (ed.), *The Apostolic Fathers*, trans. J.B. Lightfoot and J.R. Hammer, 2nd edn, Grand Rapids: Baker Book House, 1989, p. 117.

5   Edward Schillebeeckx, *Marriage: Secular Reality and Saving Mystery* Vol. II, trans. N.D. Smith, London: Sheed and Ward, 1965 [Dutch orig.: *Het huwelijk: aardse werkelijkheid en heilsmysterie*, Bilthoven: Nelissen, 1963], p. 280.

6   Heinrich Denzinger, *Enchiridion Symbolorum: Compendium of Creeds, Definitions, and Declarations on Matters of Faith and Morals*, 43rd edn, ed. Peter Hünermann, Robert Fastiggi and Anne Englund Nash, San Francisco: Ignatius Press, 2012, 1601.

7   This is still the legal position. Interestingly, earlier drafts of the Council in this regard proposed that three witnesses were required for a valid marriage, without specifying that one of them should be a priest.

8   It was St Peter Damian OSB (c.1007–72) who had proposed the consecration of virgins and the anointing of kings as sacraments.

9   Schillebeeckx, *Marriage: Secular Reality and Saving Mystery*, p. 330.

10   The term *sensus fidelium* means that the faithful have a sense of the faith. The Vatican II document on the Church in the modern world uses the term *sensus christianus fidelium* in relation to marriage and family life, which is translated in English as 'the Christian instincts of the faithful'. See *Gaudium et Spes*, 52, in Austin Flannery OP (ed.), *Vatican Council II: The Conciliar and Post Conciliar Documents*, Dublin: Dominican Publications, 1975, p. 957.

11   Schillebeeckx, *Marriage: Secular Reality and Saving Mystery*, pp. 393–4.

12   Council of Chalcedon, in Henry Bettenson (ed.), *Documents of the Christian Church*, Oxford: Oxford University Press, 1947, p. 73.

13   See Kasper, *Theology of Christian Marriage*, p. 1.

14   *Gaudium et Spes*, 48.

15   Kasper, *Theology of Christian Marriage*, p. 17.

16   Ceslas Spicq, *Lexique théologique du Nouveau Testament* (Paris: Cerf, 1991), pp. 18–33. See also C.S. Lewis, *The Four Loves*, London: Collins, Fontana Books, 1960.

17   Fintan Gavin, 'Canon 1063: Marriage Preparation as a Lifetime Journey', *Studia Canonica*, Vol. 39, (2005), pp. 181–201.

18   Vatican II, *Lumen Gentium*, 1964, 11.

19   Pope Benedict XVI, *Sacramentum Caritatis*, 2007, 27.

CHAPTER SEVEN

THE SACRAMENT
OF PRIESTHOOD

INTRODUCTION

The title 'sacrament of priesthood' most likely conjures up the image of the priest who celebrates Mass and the sacraments. But that is only part of the picture. We suggest that there is only one priesthood, the priesthood of Christ, and people share in it in two ways: through baptism and through ordination. All the baptised share in the priesthood of Christ, though this is a gift of baptism that is rarely appreciated and, in fact, remains largely unknown. Within this constituency there is a group of men who are 'ordained' priests. We term this the 'ministerial priesthood' to distinguish it from the priesthood of the baptised. We need to articulate what is distinctive about these two priesthoods and why both are necessary.

If every baptised Christian shares in the priesthood of Christ, what, then, is the ministerial or ordained priesthood? How did it develop over the centuries? What are its scriptural roots? The Second Vatican Council made clear the role and function of the bishop. It also highlighted the vocation and dignity of the priesthood of the baptised: the call to holiness of the laity. The Council had less to say about the priest, however, or so it seems.

Jesus never referred to himself as a priest. The gospels did not speak of Jesus as a priest; neither did St Paul. It is very significant that Jesus was not thought of in terms of priesthood, given that the Jewish priesthood played such an important role in the religion into which he was born. In the Synoptics we find that Jesus refers to priests in a way that is respectful of their role. He tells the leper, whom he has cured, to show himself to the priests (Mk 1:44). Leprosy was regarded as an impurity rather than a disease, and priests were expected to supervise the sanitary condition of lepers (Lev 13–14). Jesus acknowledges the authority of the priest in that regard, though he has broken the law of purity by touching the leper, albeit to cure him. Jesus comes across here as superior to the Jewish priests who cannot cure the leper. But Jesus does not refer to himself as a priest; neither does anybody else. Interestingly, he is readily regarded as a prophet. The only New Testament source that explicitly treated of Christ as priest is the Letter to the Hebrews. In doing so it relied heavily on the understanding of the priesthood in the Old Testament, though it transformed it radically. The author of Hebrews sees some similarities between Jesus and the Jewish priesthood, but his emphasis is much more on what distinguishes them. He relies very much on the figure of Melchizedek to highlight the uniqueness of the priesthood of Christ and the way in which it was different from the Jewish priesthood. Here we will examine the Letter to the Hebrews but, first of all, we will look to the source used by the unknown author of that letter: the Old Testament.

CHARACTER OF ISRAELITE PRIESTHOOD

Priestly functions, such as offering sacrifice, were originally performed by patriarchs, as heads of families or tribal groups. Gradually, these functions were subsumed by the tribe of Levi, which gave rise to the Levitical priesthood (Ex 32). The priests of the Old Testament would trace their origin to Aaron, who was of that tribe. The tribe of Levi was without territory and this lack of worldliness became an important part of the spirituality of their priests. There were Levites as well as priests, but the Levite was of lower rank than the priest and probably looked after the sanctuaries. Eventually a third rank of clergy emerged in the person of the high priest. As high priest, Joshua was a priest king, a substitute for the Davidic king.[1] The term *kohen* (priest) is probably rooted in the verb 'to find' and by extension the word 'priest' means to find oneself in the presence of the divine.

In Israelite theology the whole people was worthy of the title, 'kingdom of priests, holy nation' (Ex 19:6; see 1 Pt 2:9). But there was also a specialised priesthood. The Levitical priesthood was not a vocation or charism: people were born into it. The prophet, judge and king were regarded as having charisms, but priesthood was inherited.

The ideal of sanctity was prized in the Levitical priesthood: the priest was sanctified for and by his work. Holiness was the ideal for all the people: 'You shall be holy, for I the Lord your God am holy' (Lev 19:2). That call was addressed in a special way to priests: 'You shall treat them as holy, since they offer the food of your God; they shall be holy to you, for I the Lord, I who sanctify you, am holy' (Lev 21:8). The sanctity of the priest was considered as the holiness of separation. Just as God was other and separate, the priest should also be a man apart. Much weight was given to his separation from the secular and the profane, especially when exercising priestly service at the sanctuary. The cleanliness and purity of the priest were very much expected when he was offering sacrifice.

We need to be careful when looking at Old Testament aspects of priesthood, however, because we run the risk of assuming that what we find there is somehow a model for Christian priesthood. We need to read the Old Testament critically. This is especially true in relation to the kind of priestly spirituality that we find there. A holiness of separation is not the spirituality of the Christian priesthood, which is meant to be a spirituality of incarnation. It is in and through their pastoral relationships with people that priests are meant to live out their priesthood. They are expected to come home 'smelling of the sheep', not to remain apart, dressed in clerical finery waiting for the people to come to them. The diocesan priest is not a monk.

In his second book of the trilogy on Jesus of Nazareth, Pope Benedict XVI comments on the call to sanctification in the priestly prayer of Jesus.[2] He emphasises that sanctity is not a withdrawal from the secular and profane but is a commitment to mission. He writes as follows:

> The process of consecration, 'sanctification', includes two apparently opposed, but in reality deeply conjoined, aspects. On the one hand, 'consecrating' as 'sanctifying' means setting apart from the rest of reality ... But this setting apart also includes the essential dynamic of 'existing for'. Precisely

because it is entirely given over to God, this reality is now there for the world, for [people], it speaks for them and exists for their healing. We may also say: setting apart and mission form a single whole.[3]

FUNCTION OF THE LEVITICAL PRIEST

At that time the Lord set apart the tribe of Levi to carry the ark of the covenant of the Lord, to stand before the Lord to minister to him, and to bless in his name, to this day. Therefore Levi has no allotment or inheritance with his kindred; the Lord is his inheritance, as the Lord your God promised him. (Deut 10:8-9)

The tribe of Levi is given four responsibilities in this passage: the priests are to carry the ark of the covenant; they are to stand in the presence of the Lord; they are to serve the Lord and minister to him; and they are to bless the people in his name and call them to repentance and conversion. Three further functions can be posited. People looked to the priest to disclose God's will to them, a role that the prophets later took over. In addition, the priest had the responsibility of instructing the people in the Law: 'Then Moses and the levitical priests spoke to all Israel, saying: Keep silence and hear, O Israel! This very day you have become the people of the Lord your God' (Deut 27:9). This role was eventually taken over by the scribes. Finally, the important function of offering sacrifice came to the fore after the Babylonian exile, i.e. post 538 BCE. The priest acted as a mediator between God and his people: 'The various priestly duties share the common basis of mediation: in oracles and instruction, the priest represents God to the people; in sacrifice and intercession, he represents the people to God.'[4] Again, one has to be careful when interpreting the Old Testament understanding of priesthood. The Catholic priest is not a mediator between God and people. He is, rather, the sacrament of Christ the Mediator, as will be explained later in this chapter.

THE PRIESTHOOD OF CHRIST

Though Jesus never used the title 'priest' of himself, the gospel writers and Paul assume the priesthood of Christ in so many different ways. The preaching, healing, forgiveness and intercession of Jesus are indicators of his priesthood. The feeding of the multitude points ahead to the action of Jesus at the Last Supper. Mark, for example, presents this miracle in a way that is similar to his presentation of the Last Supper, using the four verbs: take, bless, break and give:

Mark 6:41	Mark 14:22
Taking the five loaves and the two fish, he looked up to heaven, and **blessed** and **broke** the loaves, and **gave** them to his disciples to set before the people.	While they were eating, he **took** a loaf of bread, and after **blessing** it he **broke** it, and **gave** it to them.

It was at the Last Supper that Jesus finally unveiled himself as the priest of the new covenant. The breaking of the bread anticipates the breaking of his body; the pouring of the wine similarly foreshadows the shedding of his blood.

Jesus presents himself as the new temple in the dialogue that ensued after the cleansing of the temple:

> The Jews then said to him, 'What sign can you show us for doing this?' Jesus answered them, 'Destroy this temple, and in three days I will raise it up.' The Jews then said, 'This temple has been under construction for forty-six years, and will you raise it up in three days?' But he was speaking of the temple of his body. (Jn 2:18-21)

To the Samaritan woman Jesus announces that God will be worshipped in 'spirit and truth', meaning that he himself is the locus of worship (Jn 4:23).

An important image of sacrifice in the Fourth Gospel is the lamb. John the Baptist says of Jesus: 'Here is the Lamb of God who takes away the sin of the world!' (Jn 1:29). This mysterious comment is unveiled later in the gospel when John presents the death of Jesus as taking place on Preparation Day at the hour when the lambs are being slaughtered for Passover (Jn 19:14). In the Synoptic Gospels the death of Jesus takes place on the day following the Passover. For John, Jesus is the Passover lamb. He is the sacrificial lamb but is also the priest who offers the sacrifice: he is at once priest and victim. St Paul too refers to Christ as the paschal lamb: 'For our paschal lamb, Christ, has been sacrificed' (1 Cor 5:7).

Paul is a rich source for understanding Christ's sacrifice and priesthood. The language of 1 Corinthians 10 recognises the sacrifice of Christ in the separation of his body and blood: 'The cup of blessing that we bless, is it not a sharing in the blood of Christ? The bread that we break, is it not a sharing in the body of Christ?' (1 Cor 10:16). The language of sacrifice implies the language of priesthood, though, as in the four gospels, Paul never uses the term 'priest' of Christ. We have already seen in Paul's institution narrative that he sees Christ as offering a sacrificial meal at the Last Supper, symbolic of his impending violent death.

Furthermore, in the Letter to the Romans, Paul understands the death of Christ as a sacrifice and relates it to the Jewish feast of expiation or atonement (Yom Kippur). This is the annual feast remembering when the high priest went into the Holy of Holies on his own to sprinkle sacrificial blood on the mercy seat to make atonement for his own sins and the sins of the people (Lev 16:15-17). The mercy seat covered the ark of the covenant. Christ is the new mercy seat, and it is his own blood that expiates the sins of the world. It does not take place in private but in the public arena of the hill of Calvary. The relevant passage from Paul is in chapter 3 of Romans: 'They are now justified by his grace as a gift, through the redemption that is in Christ Jesus, whom God put forward as a sacrifice of atonement by his blood, effective through faith' (Rm 3:24-5). Unlike the Old Testament expiation ritual where the initiative lay with man, the initiative in the new dispensation comes from God: God sent his own son to be the 'sacrifice of atonement'. We will see the imagery and meaning of the Day of Atonement playing a very important part in the theology of priesthood in the Letter to the Hebrews.

LETTER TO THE HEBREWS

What we have seen of the priesthood of Christ so far has been gleaned from what is implied in the gospels and the letters of St Paul. We now turn to the one explicit scriptural source for an exposition of Christ the Priest. This document, by an unknown author, was most likely written in the late 50s or early 60s CE. It is a written sermon directed to a Jewish community in Rome. The author is obviously Jewish and manifests a close familiarity with the Old Testament in its Greek translation. The Letter to the Hebrews calls Christ a priest (*hiereus*) six times and high priest (*archiereus*) ten times. His priesthood is not inherited as was the Levitical priesthood, and the two are as different as night and day. I believe this is the reason Jesus is not called a priest elsewhere nor, for that reason, does he assume the title himself. The term 'priest' as used in the Old Testament would be misleading for the kind of priest Jesus is. We need to see what Hebrews says:

> So also Christ did not glorify himself in becoming a high priest, but was appointed by the one who said to him, 'You are my Son, today I have begotten you'; as he says also in another place, 'You are a priest forever, according to the order of Melchizedek.' (Heb 5:5-6; see also 5:10; 6:20)

The two quotations within this extract are from Psalm 2 and Psalm 110 respectively. Christ did not take this honour on himself but was chosen by God. As a result of an oath (Ps 110:4) Christ is made a priest forever (Heb 7:20-21). We cannot suggest that at a particular time Christ became a priest: he was so from the moment of his incarnation. In presenting Christ as a priest 'according to the order of Melchizedek', the author of Hebrews is saying that Christ is prior to and greater than the Levitical priesthood. Melchizedek is a type of Christ. This is the import of the presentation at the beginning of chapter 7 of the Letter to the Hebrews, which is taken from the book of Genesis:

> This 'King Melchizedek of Salem, priest of the Most High God, met Abraham as he was returning from defeating the kings and blessed him'; and to him Abraham apportioned 'one-tenth of everything'. His name, in the first place, means 'king of righteousness'; next he is also king of Salem, that is, 'king of peace'. Without father, without mother, without genealogy, having neither beginning of days nor end of life, but resembling the Son of God, he remains a priest forever. (Heb 7:1-3)

There are two references to Melchizedek in the Old Testament: Genesis 14:17-20 and Psalm 110:4. *Melek* means king and *sedek* means

SACRAMENTS IN A SYNODAL CHURCH

justice; he is the king of justice or righteousness. Chapter 7 of Hebrews establishes the superiority and anteriority of Melchizedek over Levi. Abraham, of whom Levi is a descendent, pays a tithe to this king of Salem. The promise made in Psalm 110 is fulfilled in Christ: 'The Lord has sworn and will not change his mind, "You are a priest forever according to the order of Melchizedek"' (Ps 110:4). Christ's priesthood inaugurates a new law, a better covenant:

> Nor was it to offer himself again and again, as the high priest enters the Holy Place year after year with blood that is not his own; for then he would have had to suffer again and again since the foundation of the world. But as it is, he has appeared once for all at the end of the age to remove sin by the sacrifice of himself. (Heb 9:25-6)

Christ is presented here as both priest and victim or sacrifice. There is no need of further sacrifices; sin has finally been overcome. In this he contrasts with the Levitical priests who had to offer sacrifices every day. We can also refer back to the Day of Atonement mentioned above. As Fr Thomas Lane CM (1928–2011) points out, the basic typology of the Letter to the Hebrews derives from what happened on the Day of Atonement.[5] Chapter 9 of Hebrews uses the language and imagery of Leviticus 16 to show the difference between Christ and the Jewish high priest:

> But when Christ came as a high priest of the good things that have come, then through the greater and perfect tent (not made with hands, that is, not of this creation), he entered once for all into the Holy Place, not with the blood of goats and calves, but with his own blood, thus obtaining eternal redemption. (Heb 9:11-12)

The Jewish priests were continually sacrificing animals and then, once a year, the high priest went into the Holy of Holies to expiate their own sins and the sins of the people. Henceforth, none of this would be needed.

Chapter 9 goes on to speak of the new covenant inaugurated by Christ's sacrifice, a covenant of which he is mediator: 'For this reason he is the mediator of a new covenant' (Heb 9:15; see also 12:24). Salvation is assured by Christ, who can never lose his priesthood. His priesthood now consists of making intercession: 'Consequently he is able for all time to save those who approach God through him, since he always lives to make intercession for them' (Heb 7:25).[6]

Though there is no explicit mention of the Eucharist in Hebrews, reference to the 'new covenant' would resonate with a first-century audience familiar with the celebration of the Eucharist. Neither is there reference to the priesthood of the baptised or the ministerial priesthood. Hebrews is concerned only with the priesthood of Christ. Now we turn to the scriptural sources for the priesthood of the baptised. Again, it is implied rather than made explicit, as we found with the priesthood of Christ in the gospels and Pauline letters.

PRIESTHOOD OF THE BAPTISED

Two passages in Romans suggest that Christian living is a priestly sacrifice. All the baptised are called to share in the death and resurrection of Christ, to enter into the paschal mystery, becoming part of Christ's sacrifice:

> Do you not know that all of us who have been baptised into Christ Jesus were baptised into his death? Therefore we have been buried with him by baptism into death, so that, just as Christ was raised from the dead by the glory of the Father, so we too might walk in newness of life. (Rm 6:3-4)

Through baptism our whole life becomes an active participation in this paschal mystery. Further on in the Letter to the Romans, Paul makes the idea of the Christian life as a priestly sacrifice more explicit:

> I appeal to you therefore, brothers and sisters, by the mercies of God, to present your bodies as a living sacrifice, holy and acceptable to God, which is your spiritual worship. (Rm 12:1)

Sacrifice implies priesthood. The term 'bodies' is not one's physical reality but one's whole existence. For Paul, Christians live a priestly existence. We find a similar interpretation in 1 Peter:

> But you are a chosen race, a royal priesthood, a holy nation,
> God's own people, in order that you may proclaim the mighty
> acts of him who called you out of darkness into his marvellous
> light. (1 Pt 2:9)

This quotation recalls Exodus 19:6 and is the principal scriptural basis for our understanding of the priesthood of the baptised.

We find this same suggestion in the Book of Revelation. The final book of the Bible highlights the image of the lamb for Christ, which it uses twenty-seven times, though it does not use the term priest in his regard.[7] However, it refers to the saints on earth and the martyrs in heaven as priests: 'To him who loves us and freed us from our sins by his blood, and made us to be a kingdom, priests serving his God and Father, to him be glory and dominion forever and ever' (Rv 1:5-6). The heavenly liturgy in the Book of Revelation is modelled on the temple liturgy. O'Collins and Jones summarise:

> [The Book of] Revelation applies priestly language to the
> faithful, who have been made fit, even on earth, to join in the
> heavenly liturgy of praise and worship offered to God and the
> Lamb. They have been made priestly kings or kingly priests
> who serve God (5:9).[8]

According to ressourcement theologian Henri de Lubac, this language is not metaphorical: 'It is not a priesthood-on-the-cheap, a priesthood of inferior rank or a priesthood of the faithful *merely*; it is the priesthood of the whole Church.'[9]

The priesthood of the baptised, rooted in scripture, has been articulated in official documents of the Church, both ancient and modern. Fifth-century pope St Leo the Great had a developed sense of the priesthood arising from baptism:

> In baptism the sign of the cross makes kings of all who
> are reborn in Christ, and the anointing of the Holy Spirit
> consecrates them priests. So, apart from the particular
> obligations of our ministry, any Christian who has the gifts
> of rational and of spiritual understanding knows he is a
> member of a kingly race and shares in the priestly office.[10]

Pope John Paul II, in his apostolic letter on the laity, *Christifideles Laici*, states: 'The lay faithful participate, for their part, in the threefold mission of Christ as Priest, Prophet and King.'[11] Again, in *Pastores Dabo Vobis*, he reveals the mutual dependence of the priesthood of the baptised and the ministerial priesthood, given their source in Christ the Priest:

> The ministerial priesthood conferred by the sacrament of holy orders and the common or 'royal' priesthood of the faithful, which differ essentially and not only in degree, are ordered one to the other – for each in its own way derives from the one priesthood of Christ. Indeed, the ministerial priesthood does not of itself signify a greater degree of holiness with regard to the common priesthood of the faithful; through it, Christ gives to priests, in the Spirit, a particular gift so that they can help the People of God to exercise faithfully and fully the common priesthood which it has received.[12]

The Polish Pope is here echoing the teaching of Vatican II, as found in *Lumen Gentium*:

> Though they differ essentially and not only in degree, the common priesthood of the faithful and the ministerial or hierarchical priesthood are none the less interrelated; each in its own way shares in the one priesthood of Christ.[13]

The thrust of the Vatican II and post-conciliar documents is to situate the ministerial priesthood in relation to the priesthood of the baptised. While the Council of Trent, for example, properly emphasised the importance of the visible and external ministerial priesthood against the excesses of the Reformers, it did not give due recognition to the common priesthood and, from that narrow perspective, priests could see themselves as somehow above and beyond the laity.[14] This elitist thinking could also lead to an introverted clerical culture within the Church.

The *Catechism of the Catholic Church* explains the relationship between the ministerial priesthood and the priesthood of the baptised that was highlighted in *Lumen Gentium* and *Presbyterorum Ordinis*:

> While the common priesthood of the faithful is exercised by the unfolding of baptismal grace – a life of faith, hope and charity, a life according to the Spirit, the ministerial priesthood is at the service of the common priesthood. It is directed at the unfolding of the baptismal grace of all Christians. The ministerial priesthood is a *means* by which Christ unceasingly builds up and leads his Church. For this reason it is transmitted by its own sacrament, the sacrament of Holy Orders. (*CCC*, 1547)

These documents make clear that the ministerial priesthood is at the service of the baptismal priesthood. Its purpose is to enable the baptised to reach the goal for which they were created, namely to be full members of the kingdom of God in this life and in the next. Ministerial priests enable them to achieve this goal through building up the community of the Church, especially through the sacraments, the Eucharist being the 'source and summit' of the sacramental life of the Church.[15] Furthermore, all ordained priests and bishops are still part of the priesthood of the baptised.

Another way of expressing the relationship is that while all are members of the Mystical Body, not all have the same function. *Presbyterorum Ordinis*, following Trent, highlights the offering of sacrifice and the forgiveness of sins as being the main functions of the ministerial priest. The bishops are those to whom the mission of Christ has been entrusted. They are 'sharers in his consecration and mission'.[16] Priests share 'in a lesser degree' in their ministry: they are 'co-workers of the episcopal order'.[17] They share in the office of priest, prophet and king for the benefit of the Body of Christ. Through the anointing of the Holy Spirit, in a special sacrament, priests are conformed to Christ and can act 'in the person of Christ the Head.'[18] Pope Pius XII, in his encyclical *Mediator Dei* (1947), stressed that the distinctive feature of the ministerial priesthood is that it represents Christ the Head of his Body, the Church.[19]

An article written in 1975 by the French scripture scholar, and later rector of the Pontifical Biblical Institute, Albert Vanhoye (1923–2021) teases out the implications of the teaching of Vatican II on the priesthood.[20] He opines that the ministerial priesthood is subordinate to the priesthood of the baptised. It is not just the priest who offers the

Mass but all the baptised, though the ministry of the priest is essential. The reason for this is that it is Christ the Priest who brings about the Eucharist and the priest is his instrument. Vanhoye proposes that the ministerial priest is the sign and instrument of Christ the Mediator between God and people. In other words, the ordained priest is the sacrament of Christ the Mediator. He prefers this designation to that of seeing the priest as representing Christ the Head, which he fears may be interpreted in an authoritarian way.

THE MINISTERIAL PRIESTHOOD

Bishops are the successors of the apostles. The diocesan bishop is the guarantor of the unity of faith and doctrine. Priests are bound together hierarchically with the bishop: 'And so in a certain way they make him present in every congregation.'[21] The main Vatican II document on the relationship of bishop and priest is *Lumen Gentium* and, in particular, paragraph 28, where it states: 'They render the bishop present, in a way, in individual local communities'. However, the distinction between bishop and priest must be maintained. As Aidan Nichols OP points out, priesthood does not accrue from the bishop but from Christ: 'The presbyterate is not something unfolded from out of the episcopate. It is an order existing alongside the episcopate, and in its own right.'[22] This point is further underlined in the *Catechism of the Catholic Church*: 'The ministerial priesthood is a *means* by which Christ unceasingly builds up and leads his Church. For this reason it is transmitted by its own sacrament, the sacrament of Holy Orders' (*CCC*, 1547). Following the Letter to the Hebrews, *Lumen Gentium* defines priests as follows:

> In virtue of the sacrament of order, they are consecrated, in the likeness of Christ, high and eternal priest, as genuine priests of the New Testament, for the work of preaching the gospel, tending the faithful and celebrating divine worship.[23]

What is referred to in this definition are the three Christological *munera* (gifts) of sanctification, teaching and governance, based on Christ who is priest, prophet and king, though they are expressed in a different order in this quotation. While there are hints of the *munus triplex* (triple gift) in the patristic period, the systematic use of the term can be traced to the Reformation. It was later borrowed from the Lutherans by German-speaking Catholic theologians in the eighteenth century. John Henry Newman (1801–90) used the term also, taking it from Calvin's *Institutes*. The three *munera* of the priesthood are mentioned for the first time in official documents of the Church in Pope Pius XII's encyclicals *Mystici Corporis Christi* (1943) and *Mediator Dei* (1947).

We will now reflect on each of the *munera*, using the language of the *Lumen Gentium*: preaching the gospel, tending the faithful and celebrating divine worship. The mission of Christ as priest, prophet and king is continued in the Church by the ministerial priesthood and by the priesthood of the baptised. In the following exploration of these three gifts we need to keep in mind that all the baptised have the privilege and responsibility to preach the gospel, tend the faithful and celebrate divine worship. The function of the ordained priest will differ in certain ways, especially in the celebration of the sacraments, but it is the Church as a whole that carries out the mission of Christ. We will examine how the *tria munera* are exercised in the Church from the perspective of the ministerial priest, but realising that this must take place in conjunction with all the baptised.

Preaching the Gospel

In St Mark's account of the calling of the apostles, three reasons are presented as motivating the call – they are called to be with Jesus, to preach and to cast out devils:

> He went up the mountain and called to him those whom he wanted, and they came to him. And he appointed twelve, whom he also named apostles, to be with him, and to be sent out to proclaim the message, and to have authority to cast out demons. (Mk 3:13-15)

Presbyterorum Ordinis emphasises that preaching is the first duty of the priest: 'Priests, as co-workers with their bishops, have the primary duty of proclaiming the Gospel of God to all.'[24] Proclamation of the Word is essential in the celebration of the sacraments to awaken and develop the faith of the participants, thereby deepening the reception of the sacraments on the part of the participant, especially the Eucharist: 'The Eucharist shows itself as the source and summit of the whole work of preaching the Gospel.'[25] The prophetic and priestly roles are closely connected in that it is the sacrifice of Christ that gives effectiveness to the ministerial priesthood and the priesthood of the baptised.

Tending the Faithful

Presbyterorum Ordinis opens with a strong emphasis on the ministerial priesthood as a service to the priesthood of the baptised; it is not a privilege bestowed on a few for their own benefit. The Vatican II document on seminary formation, *Optatam Totius*, reminds students of the importance of having the right intention: 'The students should understand most clearly that they are not destined for domination or for honours but are given over totally to the service of God and to the pastoral ministry.'[26] Great harm has been done in parishes where priests belittled people and alienated them from the Church. A humbler Church is to be welcomed.

Presbyterorum Ordinis raises the question of the relationship of the priest to people. Priests need to be in close contact with people if they are to fulfil their function. Unlike the monk, the diocesan priest cannot afford himself the luxury of being a man apart. Following the example of Christ, who came among us as a man, the priest needs to develop real relationships with people: 'They cannot be of service to [people] if they remain strangers to the life and conditions of [people].'[27] While not conforming to the world, priests need to be in the world. Just as Christ became man in a certain time and place, so the priest leaves his family and friends and makes his home in a parish, or hospital, or college and becomes an *alter Christus* ('another Christ') in this new community. There he will reach out to people of all ages and conditions, having a 'special obligation' to the 'poor and weak', 'youth', 'married people and parents', 'the sick and the dying', the lonely, those overburdened with work and exiles.[28] *Lumen Gentium*, for its part, highlights the importance of seeking out the lost. As 'good shepherds' priests should 'search out even those who, after baptism in the Catholic Church, have fallen away from sacramental practice, or, worse still, from belief.'[29]

Throughout the text, *Presbyterorum Ordinis* continues to highlight the necessity of a proper relationship between priests and laity: 'Priests must sincerely acknowledge and promote the dignity of the laity and the part proper to them in the mission of the Church. And they should hold in high honour that just freedom which is due to everyone in the earthly city.'[30] This will involve listening to the laity and recognising their competencies in the life of the Church. In parishes nowadays the priest works closely with several groups of lay people, especially the parish council or assembly and the finance committee. This is a very practical expression of synodality.

The document *Optatam Totius* calls on the seminarian to develop an ability to dialogue with people: 'Correctly understanding the characteristics of the contemporary mind, [they] will be duly prepared for dialogue with [people] of their time.'[31] The priest needs to remember that he is among his people as one who serves, after the example of his Master.

From the very beginning of his seminary formation the seminarian should seek to find a road map to holiness and human maturity. These are the pillars on which a fruitful priestly ministry is built. Exhorting priests to the highest degree of holiness, *Presbyterorum Ordinis* recognises that the life and activity of priesthood lead to holiness: 'Priests who perform their duties sincerely and indefatigably in the Spirit of Christ arrive at holiness by this very fact.'[32] In the words of the Congregation for the Clergy, 'it is a holiness in ministry and through ministry'.[33] Aidan Nichols OP has an interesting comment on the same lines: 'The presbyter, unlike the monk, cannot be wholly occupied in contemplation. His is a public mission in the Church: his service to other human beings, and not simply his participation in the heavenly choir, renders him "angelic".'[34] Pastoral work, then, is not a distraction from the spiritual life but is part of it.

Human maturity is sometimes markedly lacking in some priests, to the detriment of their ministry. Immaturity in a priest expresses itself in noticeably seeking attention; using tragedy in the lives of parishioners to make himself the centre of attention; the emotional exploitation of people and liturgies – especially at funeral Masses; a tendency to talk about himself in his homilies; the use of coarse language; a tendency to criticise his superiors (parish priest/bishop) in a silly kind of way; developing exclusive relations with individuals or families in his parish or manifesting an inability to care for people. Lack of care shows itself, for example, when a priest forgets an important detail about a parishioner, like a serious illness. A priest too will say he is no good at names, but he may have no problem memorising the vocabulary of a foreign language! An immature priest is a big turn off for people, especially the young. He certainly undermines vocation promotion. Every effort should be made in the seminary to develop human and spiritual maturity. This involves taking seriously the advice of spiritual directors or formation personnel and making a serious attempt to integrate advice and criticism. The lives of the saints offer plenty of evidence of very saintly people who were excessive in their prayer or penance but who obeyed the advice of their directors. Obedience to God finds its practical expression in obedience to our ecclesiastical superiors: 'In a great spirit of faith, let them receive and execute whatever orders the Holy Father, their own bishop, or other superiors give or recommend.'[35]

Celebrating Divine Worship

In *Presbyterorum Ordinis* we read: 'Priests act especially in the person of Christ as ministers of holy things, particularly in the Sacrifice of the Mass'.[36] The conciliar and post-conciliar documents highlight the Eucharist as the supreme Christian act: 'The liturgy is the summit towards which the activity of the Church is directed; it is also the font from which all her power flows.'[37] Similar statements can be found in two other documents of the Council. *Lumen Gentium* describes the Eucharist as the 'source and summit of the entire Christian life'.[38] The idea of the Eucharist as summit of the Christian life is found too in the *Summa Theologiae,* as we have already noted. St Thomas Aquinas sees baptism as the beginning of the spiritual life and the Eucharist as its summit: 'Baptism is the beginning of the spiritual life and the door of the sacraments; whereas the Eucharist is, as it were, the consummation of the spiritual life and the goal of all the sacraments'.[39]

The self-giving of the priest to his people draws its inspiration and strength from the Eucharist: 'Pastoral charity flows out in a very special way from the Eucharistic sacrifice. This stands as the root and centre of the whole life of a priest.'[40]

Following the conciliar and post-conciliar documents we have seen that the ministerial priesthood derives from the priesthood of Christ. The priest represents the bishop who is the successor of the apostles and the source of unity in a diocese, unity of faith and teaching. The function of the priest is to serve the priesthood of the baptised so that they may become a holy priesthood acceptable to the Lord. The three *munera* of sanctification, teaching and governance that we saw defined in *Lumen Gentium* earlier mark the life and ministry of the priest.

NOT A SEAMLESS SUCCESSION

Many presume that there was a seamless succession from apostles to bishops and these, in turn, ordained priests. The evidence in scripture and in early Christian writing, however, does not support this view. To dip into this evidence it is necessary to use some Greek terms: *episkopos*, *presbuteros* and *diakonos*. *Episkopos* identifies someone who has oversight or exercises a supervisory role. *Presbuteros* literally means an elder, but it does not imply an older person: it refers to someone who has authority. *Diakonos* connotes someone who serves. These terms will eventually be translated as bishop, priest and deacon, respectively.

The titles *episkopos* and *presbuteros* are used interchangeably in the New Testament, though some other terms with similar connotations are also used. There is some confusion as to the precise nature of the different ministers that were present in the early Christian communities. In First Thessalonians, Paul refers to *proistamenoi en tô Kuriô*, literally 'presidents in the Lord', translated as those who 'have charge of you in the Lord' (1 Th 5:12). Another general term is found in Hebrews: *hêgoumenoi* (leaders): 'Remember your leaders, those who spoke the word of God to you' (Heb 13:7). These terms may be identified with presbyters, or presbyters with *episkopê* (oversight, supervision). The difference between *presbuteros* and *episkopos* is not clear-cut. It is possible that communities were governed by colleges of presbyters who possessed *episkopê*. Presbyters had an active share in organising Church life, unlike the deacons who were dependent on the *episkopoi*.[41]

In the post-Pauline churches, presbyters and bishops were practically one and the same: as a group they were responsible for the pastoral care of the churches. The pastoral epistles, 1 Peter and Acts describe their character and activities in the 80s CE, if not earlier (1 Tm 3:1-7; Ti 1:7-9). While the apostle moved from place to place in a missionary way, the presbyter-bishop remained in the area for which he was responsible. In this sense the latter was more an institutional figure.

In Acts, Paul's farewell speech to the presbyters of the church of Ephesus reveals that a group of presbyters were responsible for the pastoral care of that community:

> Keep watch over yourselves and over all the flock, of which the Holy Spirit has made you overseers, to shepherd the church of God that he obtained with the blood of his own

Son. I know that after I have gone, savage wolves will come in among you, not sparing the flock. (Acts 20:28-9)

It is reasonable to conclude from this statement that the Church at the time believed that pastoral authority had been transmitted from the apostles to the presbyters who were carrying out the apostles' work. Evidence for the theory that the Church was governed by a group of presbyters rather than one individual (bishop) is further gleaned from the First Letter of Peter:

So I exhort the presbyters among you, as a fellow presbyter and witness to the sufferings of Christ and one who has a share in the glory to be revealed. Tend [*poimanate*] the flock of God in your midst, [overseeing [*episkopountes*]] not by constraint but willingly, as God would have it, not for shameful profit but eagerly. Do not lord it over those assigned to you, but be examples to the flock. And when the chief Shepherd is revealed, you will receive the unfading crown of glory. Likewise, you younger members, be subject to the presbyters. (1 Pt 5:1-5)[42]

In the second line here, the verb *poimainein* means 'to tend' or 'to shepherd'. The quotation implies that presbyters were shepherds of the flock, exercising oversight (*episkopountes*).

Towards the end of the first century we find Ignatius of Antioch attesting to the presence of a bishop in Ephesus and Antioch, together with a college of presbyters. However, in his letter to Polycarp we find mention of deacons and presbyters at Philippi but no reference to a bishop. There was probably no bishop in Philippi at that time. One can conclude that the episcopate developed sooner in Syria and Asia Minor than it did in Europe. Francis Sullivan SJ (1922–2019) brings together the different positions of Ignatius and Polycarp in this cogent remark:

Whereas Ignatius called on Christians to be subject to the bishop as to God and Christ and to the presbyters as to the apostles, Polycarp calls for obedience to the presbyters and the deacons as to God and Christ.[43]

By the end of the second century each church was led by a bishop and these bishops were understood to be the successors of the apostles.

In summary, we can conclude that Jesus did not give a blueprint for ministry in the Church, as several questions remained. He did not have a mission to the Gentiles: should they be part of the mission of the apostles? Should these be obliged to follow the Mosaic law before being baptised? What structure should be put in place? Was a structure necessary at all given that Jesus was expected to return soon? In the Acts of the Apostles, we find that the apostles faced each question in turn and relied on the Holy Spirit in conjunction with consultations among themselves. This synodal approach was especially evident in chapter 15 where the apostles had to decide whether to make circumcision obligatory for Gentile converts. So while Jesus did not give a blueprint for so many issues, his followers were inspired to trust in their own deliberations once they were open to the guidance of the Holy Spirit. Raymond Brown PSS (1928–98) sums up the human and divine elements involved in the development of the Church:

> I am not so naïve to think that every development within the Church is the work of the Spirit; but I would not know what guidance of the Church by the Spirit could mean if it did not include the fundamental shaping of the special ministry which is so intimately concerned with Christian communal and sacramental life.[44]

Just as the Holy Spirit guided the early Church (second century) to decide on a canon of scripture, similarly the Holy Spirit guided the Church in deciding who succeeded the apostles. Their role was essential to protecting the faith from the undermining threat of Gnosticism, for example.

> Although development of church structure reflects sociological necessity, in the Christian self-understanding the Holy Spirit given by the risen Christ guides the church in such a way that allows basic structural development to be seen as embodying Jesus Christ's will for his church.[45]

While there are gaps in our knowledge of the movement from the apostles to the post-apostolic period as well as some ambiguity about terminology, by the second century a structure was in place that was regarded as in continuity with the apostolic Church. The threefold ministry of bishop, priest and deacon dates from this period.

THE PERMANENT DIACONATE

One of the recommendations proposed by the Second Vatican Council was the restoration of the permanent diaconate.[46] The diaconate played a significant role in the early centuries of the Church, but there was a parting of ways between the Western and Eastern churches from the fifth century onwards. The Western Latin Church confined the diaconate to celibate men who were near ordination to priesthood, while the Eastern Church continued to ordain men to the permanent diaconate. Interestingly, the Council of Trent had earlier proposed that the Western Church should restore the diaconate, but this did not happen until after Vatican II. Following the Second Vatican Council the restoration was gradual, with some national churches responding immediately to this request, while others waited until the present millennium. Just as in the East, both married and single men are now invited to become permanent deacons in the Catholic Church.

So what is the permanent diaconate? The diaconate has its roots in Christ, who came among us 'as one who serves' (Lk 22:27). Christ's mission and ministry are described in terms of the verb *diakoneo* ('I serve'): 'For the Son of Man came not to be served but to serve, and to give his life as a ransom for many' (Mk 10:45). Jesus' service is primarily to his Father and to the truth, carrying out God's will to the point of death. It is also directed to the poor and oppressed. Jesus' service of the truth and his compassion for the poor are intrinsically linked because it is the truth that liberates (Jn 8:32). Service too marks the institution of the Eucharist when the washing of the feet at the Last Supper is proposed as an example that Jesus wishes his disciples to imitate (Jn 13:12-15).

The *kenosis* (self-emptying) of Christ in the hymn of Philippians 2:6-11 stands as a model of the Christian life. It is quoted by Paul following the admonition, 'Let the same mind be in you that was in Christ Jesus' (Phil 2:5). It contrasts with the self-glorifying of the Roman emperors (who were thought of as being in the form of God).

All Christians, whether in ministry or not, are called to have the mind of Christ, the self-emptying, self-giving to God, leading to the *diakonia* of God's people. Therefore, all ministries must take their inspiration from Christ the servant.

What, then, is specific to the deacon? The deacon is the sacramental sign in the Church of Christ the servant. If we understand 'sacrament' as a sign that effects what it signifies (*efficiunt quod figurant*), then the deacon, in his person and his ministry, makes present 'Christ the servant'.[47] In contrast, the bishop and priest are the sacramental sign of Christ the Shepherd or Head: in their person and ministry they are *in persona Christi*.[48]

Deacons are ordained 'not unto the priesthood, but unto the ministry' (Latin: '*non ad sacerdotium, sed ad ministerium*').[49] The Fathers of the Church and the early councils refer to deacons as ministers of the Church of God. The theology of the diaconate devolves from the spiritual dynamism of the sacrament of orders and is not a further development of the theology of the laity. The diaconate, in so far as it is a grade of sacred orders, confers a character and communicates a specific sacramental grace. The deacon participates in the ministry of Christ and is the sacramental sign in the Church of Christ the Servant. Becoming a deacon is not a new way of exercising a lay ministry: 'Strengthened by sacramental grace deacons are dedicated to the people of God, in communion with the bishop and his body of priests, in the service of the liturgy, of the word and of works of charity.'[50]

In conclusion, the diaconate began in quite a fluid manner in the early Church and developed over the centuries. It still has the potential to develop and change. Current Church discipline regarding this grade of orders is heavily influenced by tradition and by a desire to imitate the discipline and practice of the diaconate in the Eastern Church.

Notes

1   In the first letter of St Clement to the Corinthians it is possible to see a parallel suggested between the three ranks of the Levitical priesthood and the priesthood of the new covenant: the high priest, the priest and the Levite may correspond to the bishop, priest and deacon. See Louis Leloir, 'Valeurs du sacerdoce lévitique' in Joseph Coppens (ed.), *Sacerdoce et célibat: Etudes historiques et théologiques, Bibliotheca Ephemeridum Theologicarum Lovaniensium*, Gembloux: Editions Duculot, 1971, p. 26: 'For to the high priest the proper services have been given, and to the priests the proper office has been assigned, and upon the Levites the proper ministries have been imposed' (*I Clement*, 40.5).

2   'Sanctify them in the truth; your word is truth. As you have sent me into the world, so I have sent them into the world. And for their sakes I sanctify myself, so that they also may be sanctified in truth' (Jn 17:17-19).

3   Pope Benedict XVI, *Jesus of Nazareth: Holy Week: From the Entrance into Jerusalem to the Resurrection*, London: CTS, 2011, p. 86.

4   Werner Dommershausen, 'kohen, priest', in G.J. Botterweck, H. Ringren, and H.-J. Fabry (eds) *Theological Dictionary of the Old Testament*, trans. D.E. Green, Vol. 7, Grand Rapids, Michigan: Eerdmans, 1995, pp. 60–75 (p. 70).

5   Thomas Lane, *Priesthood: Changeless and Changing*, Dublin: Columba Press, 2005, pp. 17–18.

6   See also Romans 8:34: 'It is Christ Jesus, who died, yes, who was raised, who is at the right hand of God, who indeed intercedes for us.'

7   Gerald O'Collins and Michael Keenan Jones, *Jesus Our Priest: A Christian Approach to the Priesthood of Christ*, Oxford: Oxford University Press, 2010, p. 39.

8   Ibid., p. 41.

9   Henri de Lubac, *The Splendor of the Church*, trans. Michael Mason, San Francisco: Ignatius Press, 1986, 1989, p. 135.

10 Pope St Leo the Great, Sermon 4, 1–2. *The Divine Office* III, London: Collins, 1974, p. 387*–8*.

11 Pope John Paul II, *Christifideles Laici*, 1988, 14.

12 Pope John Paul II, *Pastores Dabo Vobis*, 1992, 17.

13 Vatican II, *Lumen Gentium*, 1964, 10.

14 Martin Luther emphasised the inner priesthood of Christ. He did not accept that the Last Supper was a sacrifice but saw it as Christ's last will and testament. He rejected the sacrament of orders as necessary for the exercise of priesthood, claiming instead that any baptised Christian could exercise priesthood, provided they were elected to do so by the community.

15 *Lumen Gentium*, 11.

16 Vatican II, *Presbyterorum Ordinis*, 1965, 2.

17 Ibid.

18 Ibid.

19 Aidan Nichols, *Holy Order: Apostolic Priesthood from the New Testament to the Second Vatican Council*, Dublin: Veritas, 1990, p. 129.

20 Albert Vanhoye, 'Sacerdoce commun et sacerdoce ministériel', *Nouvelle Revue Théologique*, Vol. 3 (1975), pp. 193–207.

21 *Presbyterorum Ordinis*, 5.

22 Nichols, *Holy Order*, p. 136.

23 *Lumen Gentium*, 28.

24 *Presbyterorum Ordinis*, 4.

25 Ibid., 5.

26 Vatican II, *Optatam Totius*, 1965, 9.

27 *Presbyterorum Ordinis*, 3.

28 Ibid., 6, 8.

29 *Lumen Gentium*, 28.

30 *Presbyterorum Ordinis*, 9.

31 *Optatam Totius*, 15.

32 *Presbyterorum Ordinis*, 13.

33 Instruction of the Congregation for the Clergy, *The Priest, Pastor and Leader of the Parish Community*, 2002, 12.

34 Nichols, *Holy Order*, p. 114.

35 *Presbyterorum Ordinis*, 15.

36 Ibid., 13.

37 Vatican II, *Sacrosanctum Concilium*, 1963, 10.

38 *Lumen Gentium*, 11.

39 Aquinas, *Summa Theologiae*, IIIa, q. 73, a. 3, Respondeo.

40 *Presbyterorum Ordinis*, 14.

41 Nichols, *Holy Order*, p. 31.

42 From *The New American Bible (Revised Edition)*, New York: HarperCollins, 2012.

43 Francis A. Sullivan SJ, *From Apostles to Bishops: The Development of the Episcopacy in the Early Church*, New York: Newman Press, 2001, p. 128.

44 Raymond E. Brown, *Priest and Bishop: Biblical Reflections*, New York/Paramus, N.J.: Paulist Press, 1970, p. 4.

45 Raymond E. Brown, *Introduction to the New Testament*, Anchor Bible Reference Library, New York: Doubleday, 1997, p. 295.

46 *Lumen Gentium*, 29.

47 Aquinas, *Summa Theologiae*, q. 62, a. 1, ad primum.

48 *Lumen Gentium*, 28, 10.

49 Ibid., 29.

50 Ibid.

THE MISSION OF THE SYNODAL CHURCH

While challenges remain in regard to the Church and its sacraments, it is important to state that there is much to celebrate and be grateful for, as we have seen throughout this book. We do not have the privilege of knowing Jesus in his human nature as his contemporaries did, but we have the best alternative: he is accessible to us in a human, tangible way in the Church, especially through her sacraments. To open up this richness we need all our people to realise they are the people of God, part of the great communion we call Church. Participation in this communion means recognising that all the baptised share in the priesthood of Christ, i.e. in the privilege and responsibility of being priest, prophet and king. In other words, all are called to the work of sanctification (priest), preaching (prophet) and governance (king). Parents who teach their children to pray and who bring them to Mass are doing the work of sanctification. Those who explain the faith, whether it is in a formal catechetical setting or in the family, are fulfilling the prophetic role. Parishioners involved in parish councils and finance committees are exercising governance. A critical element in the functioning of the priesthood of the baptised is faith formation.

In an address to his diocese, Bishop Alan McGuckian SJ made this pertinent comment:

> It is essential for the missionary outreach of the diocese that we form ourselves in a deep knowledge of the Faith. Only people who have come to know Christ deeply as he reveals himself in Word and Sacrament will be able to proclaim Him effectively to others. Our Plan proposes a renewal of faith formation across the ages with an emphasis on children and young adults.[1]

Finally, I would like to focus on 'missionary outreach', which coincides with the third of the synodal signposts, mission. In *Evangelii Gaudium* Pope Francis emphasises the missionary dimension of the gospel on practically every page: 'All of us are asked to obey his call to go forth from our own comfort zone in order to reach all the "peripheries" in need of the light of the Gospel.'[2] He identifies gospel joy as missionary joy. He wants maintenance to give way to mission. He is calling us out of the bunker and into the trenches. This will have enormous consequence for the Church of the future. Gone are the days when mission was confined to priests and religious. All participate. Pope Francis is not saying something radically new here. He is drawing out the implications of the gospel and the documents of the Second Vatican Council. The Vatican II document on mission states that the Church is missionary 'by her very nature'.[3] The document on the Church, *Lumen Gentium*, gives the reason why this is so:

> Christ is the light of humanity; and it is, accordingly, the heart-felt desire of this sacred Council, being gathered together in the Holy Spirit, that, by proclaiming his Gospel to every creature, it may bring to all [people] that light of Christ which shines out visibly from the Church.[4]

We draw inspiration from the scriptures and the early Church. In particular, we trace the spiritual journey of the apostles from Easter Sunday to Pentecost. The resurrection confirmed that Jesus was who he had claimed to be. The disciples had certainty after the resurrection, but their fear remained. Back in Jerusalem after the ascension, they confined themselves to the upper room. There was no preaching or missionary activity. A miracle was needed to change these faith-filled but fearful followers of Jesus. The miracle was Pentecost. The promise of Jesus was fulfilled:

> You will receive power when the Holy Spirit has come upon you; and you will be my witnesses in Jerusalem, and in all Judea and Samaria, and to the ends of the earth. (Acts 1:8)

Look at the transformation in these frightened apostles. We hear their powerful preaching in the Acts of the Apostles. They were new men empowered by the Holy Spirit. And indeed they were witnesses to the point of giving their lives. St Paul too exemplifies what is possible in the Spirit. The persecutor of Christians becomes the great apostle of the Gentiles. He attributes his power to the Holy Spirit:

> For I will not venture to speak of anything except what Christ has accomplished through me to win obedience from the Gentiles, by word and deed, by the power of signs and wonders, by the power of the Spirit of God, so that from Jerusalem and as far around as Illyricum I have fully proclaimed the good news of Christ. (Rm 15:18-19)

Like the twelve apostles, Paul has received the Holy Spirit who empowers him to preach Christ in Syria and Greece despite the enormous difficulties he encountered by way of attack and gruelling journeys at sea. His three missionary journeys as recounted in Acts are truly compelling.

What Pentecost was for the apostles, the sacrament of confirmation is for all Christians, as we saw in our third chapter. We need to draw on the gifts and fruits of the Spirit that we received in that sacrament so that we have the faith conviction and the courage to be missionary. What we need is *parrhesia*. This is a word found in the Greek New Testament that means to speak plainly, to speak without fear. It also has the sense of the boldness or courage that comes from the Holy Spirit.

Parrhesia is a term much lauded by Pope Francis. He does so in his apostolic exhortation *Gaudete et Exsultate* ('Rejoice and Be Glad'), published in 2018 on the subject of holiness. He writes: 'Holiness is also *parrhesía*: it is boldness, an impulse to evangelise and to leave a mark in this world. ... Boldness, enthusiasm, the freedom to speak out, apostolic fervour, all these are included in the word *parrhesía*.'[5] *Parrhesia* is not a bullish arrogance pushing the gospel message down people's throats. It is a quiet confidence, knowing that the Spirit is at work in us and in those we encounter. The Pope describes it as 'a seal of the Spirit; it testifies to the authenticity of our preaching'.[6]

How does *parrhesia* work in practice? To illustrate I will take the example of an initiative of the French Church from which I have drawn a lot of inspiration. Over a two-year period in the mid-1990s, the French Conference of Bishops engaged in a wide consultation with groups involved in the Church throughout France. We would describe the process today as an exercise in synodality. This consultation led to the publication of a letter to the Catholics of the country in 1996 entitled *Proposer la foi dans la société actuelle: Lettre aux Catholiques de France*.[7] The message of the letter was that the Christian faith is not a cultural reality that can be imposed on people. It is, rather, a response to a gospel that is proposed to them with all the immediacy and power of the *kerygma* (apostolic teaching). One of the first quotations in the document is from Pope John Paul II's homily at Reims:

> The Church is always a Church of the present time. It doesn't see its heritage as a treasure of bygone days, but as a powerful inspiration for moving forwards in the pilgrimage of faith on roads that are always new.[8]

These words coincide with the spirit of the document, which rejects all nostalgia for the glory days of the French Church:

> We reject all nostalgia for the times in the past when the principle of authority seemed to impose itself unquestioningly. We are not dreaming of an impossible return to what was called 'Christendom'.[9]

The time for hand-wringing is past: the time has come to place the future in Christ and in the power of the gospel. The document is not suggesting a new plan that will better combat the decline in faith and practice: 'It is not a question of developing a strategy. It is a question of focusing on and deepening our involvement in faith in the God of Jesus Christ, as we live it in the communion of the Church.'[10] This is the key to synodality. It involves a rediscovery of the power of Christ in word and sacrament. The document puts its hope in Christ proclaimed and lived sacramentally in the Church. It involves going to the heart of the mystery of faith, recognising that the cause of God cannot be separated from the cause of the human person. The experience of God is not an imposition from the outside but is rooted in the religious desire in the hearts of all people. The relationship is one of freedom: there can be no imposition.

At the end of his Last Supper discourse Jesus gave the reason why he had spoken to his apostles that evening; it was so that they would have his joy: 'I have said these things to you so that my joy may be in you, and that your joy may be complete' (Jn 15:11). This surely is the reason why we write, or teach, or preach – to open up minds and hearts to the joy of Christ that comes from his Spirit. This joy is a profound sense of knowing that life has meaning and that we are loved by God. In his visit to Malta in 2022, Pope Francis connected this joy with evangelisation. Seven times during one of his homilies he repeated his conviction that 'the joy of the Church is to evangelise'.[11] May this book lead to joy, the Joy of the Gospel, *Evangelii Gaudium*.

Notes

1   Bishop Alan McGuckian SJ, Statement at the Launch of *Forward Together/ Ar Aghaidh le Chéile* Pastoral Plan for Raphoe Diocese, Maynooth: Catholic Communications Office, 31 March 2022.

2   Pope Francis, *Evangelii Gaudium*, 2013, 20.

3   Vatican II, *Ad Gentes*, 1965, 2.

4   Vatican II, *Lumen Gentium*, 1964, 1.

5   Pope Francis, *Gaudete et Exsultate*, 2018, 129.

6   Ibid., 132.

7   Les Evêques de France, *Proposer la foi dans la société actuelle: Lettre aux Catholiques de France ('Proposing the Faith in Current Society: Letter to the Catholics of France')*, Paris: Cerf, 1996.

8   Pope John Paul II, Homélie de Reims, 5, Textes intégraux, p. 111, 1996, quoted in *Proposer la foi dans la société actuelle*, p. 12. Translation my own.

9   *Proposer la foi dans la société actuelle*, p. 20. Translation my own.

10   Ibid., p. 11.

11   Pope Francis, *Homily at the National Shrine of 'Ta' Pinu' in Gozo*, 2 April 2022.

BIBLIOGRAPHY

Apostolic Penitentiary, *Note from the Apostolic Penitentiary on the Sacrament of Reconciliation in the Current Pandemic*, Vatican: Holy See Press Office, 20 March 2020.

Aquinas, T., *Somme théologique* [*Summa Theologiae*], Vols 1–3, Paris: Les Editions du Cerf, 1984-86.

Augustine, *The City of God*, Vol. 3: Books VIII–XI (Loeb Classical Library, no. 413), trans. David S. Wiesen, Cambridge: Harvard University Press, 1989.

Bettenson, H. (ed.), *Documents of the Christian Church*, Oxford: Oxford University Press, 1947.

Brown, R.E., *Priest and Bishop: Biblical Reflections*, New York/Paramus, N.J.: Paulist Press, 1970.

_____ *Introduction to the New Testament*, Anchor Bible Reference Library, New York: Doubleday, 1997.

Brugès, J.L., 'L'eucharistie et l'urgence du mystère', *Nouvelle Revue Théologique*, Vol. 130, No. 1 (2008), pp. 3–25.

Chauvet, L.M., *Symbole et Sacrement: Une relecture sacramentelle de l'existence Chrétienne*, Paris: Cerf, 1987.

Congar, Y., 'Dogme christologique et ecclésiologie. Vérité et limites d'un parallèle', in *Das Konzil von Chalkedon. Geschichte und Gegenwart*, Vol. 3, Würzburg: Echter Verlag, 1954.

Congregation for Divine Worship and the Discipline of the Sacraments, *Rediscovering the Rite of Penance*, Vatican: Libreria Editrice Vaticana, 2015.

Congregation for the Clergy, *The Priest, Pastor and Leader of the Parish Community*, Vatican: Libreria Editrice Vaticana, 2002.

Cross, F.L. and E.A. Livingstone, *The Oxford Dictionary of the Christian Church*, 2nd edn, Oxford: Oxford University Press, 1957.

De Lubac, H., *Catholicism: Christ and the Common Destiny of Man*, trans. L.C. Sheppard and E. Englund, San Francisco: Ignatius Press, 1988 [French orig.: *Catholicisme: les aspects sociaux du dogme*, Paris: Cerf, 1938, 2003].

_____ 'Causes internes de l'atténuation et de la disparition du sens du Sacré', in *Bulletin des aumôniers catholiques. Chantiers de la jeunesse*, No. 31 (1942), republished in *Theology in History*, San Francisco: Ignatius Press, 1996.

_____ *The Motherhood of the Church*, trans. S. Englund, San Francisco: Ignatius Press, 1982 [French orig.: *Les églises particulières dans l'Église universelle*, Paris: Aubier Montaigne, 1971].

_____ *The Splendor of the Church*, trans. M. Mason, San Francisco: Ignatius Press, 1986, 1989 [French orig.: *Méditation sur l'Église*, Paris: Editions Montaigne, 1953].

Denzinger, H., *Enchiridion Symbolorum: Compendium of Creeds, Definitions, and Declarations on Matters of Faith and Morals,* 43rd edn, ed. P. Hünermann, R. Fastiggi and A.E. Nash, San Francisco: Ignatius Press, 2012 [Freiburg im Breisgau: Verlag Herder, 2010].

Dictionnaire de Théologie Catholique, Paris: Librairie Letouzey et Ané, 1939.

Dommershausen, W., '*kohen*, priest', in G. J. Botterweck, H. Ringren, and H.J. Fabry (eds) *Theological Dictionary of the Old Testament*, trans. D. E. Green, Vol. 7, Grand Rapids, Michigan: Eerdmans, 1995, pp. 60–75.

Duffy, R.A., 'Baptism and Confirmation', in F. Schüssler Fiorenza and J.P. Galvin (eds) *Systematic Theology: Roman Catholic Perspectives* Volume II, Minneapolis: Fortress Press, 1991.

Dulles, A., *Models of Revelation*, Maryknoll, New York: Orbis Books, 1983, 1992, 2014.

Ernst, C., *The Theology of Grace* ('Theology Today' series, 17), Dublin and Cork: Mercier Press, 1974.

Flannery, A. (ed.), *Vatican Council II: The Conciliar and Post Conciliar Documents*, Dublin: Dominican Publications, 1975.

Gavin, F., 'Canon 1063: Marriage Preparation as a Lifetime Journey', *Studia Canonica*, Vol. 39 (2005), pp. 181–201.

Haight, R., *The Experience and Language of Grace*, New York: Paulist Press, 1979.

Hardon, J., *History and Theology of Grace*, Michigan: Veritas Press of Ave Maria College, 2002.

Henry, M., 'Reflections on Grace', 1, 2, 3, *Irish Theological Quarterly*, Vol. 66, No. 3 (2001), pp. 195– 210, Vol. 66, No. 4 (2001), pp. 295–314, Vol. 67, No. 1 (2002), pp. 55–68.

Holmes, M.W. (ed.), *The Apostolic Fathers*, trans. J.B. Lightfoot and J.R. Hammer, 2nd edition, Grand Rapids: Baker Book House, 1989.

International Theological Commission, *The Reciprocity Between Faith and Sacraments in the Sacramental Economy*, 2020.

Kasper, W., *Theology of Christian Marriage*, London: Burns & Oates, 1980.

Lane, T., *Priesthood: Changeless and Changing*, Dublin: Columba Press, 2005.

Leloir, L., 'Valeurs du Sacerdoce Lévitique' in Joseph Coppens (ed.), *Sacerdoce et célibat: Etudes historiques et théologiques, Bibliotheca Ephemeridum Theologicarum Lovaniensium*, Gembloux: Editions Duculot, 1971.

Les Evêques de France, *Proposer la foi dans la société actuelle: Lettre aux Catholiques de France*, ['*Proposing the Faith in Current Society: Letter to the Catholics of France*'], Paris: Cerf, 1996.

Lewis, C.S., *The Four Loves*, London: Collins, Fontana Books, 1960.

McGuckian, A., Statement at the Launch of *Forward Together/Ar Aghaidh le Chéile* Pastoral Plan for Raphoe Diocese, Maynooth: Catholic Communications Office, 31 March 2022.

Nichols, A., *Holy Order: Apostolic Priesthood from the New Testament to the Second Vatican Council*, Dublin: Veritas, 1990.

O'Collins, G. and M.K. Jones, *Jesus Our Priest: A Christian Approach to the Priesthood of Christ*, Oxford: Oxford University Press, 2010.

Pope Benedict XVI, *Jesus of Nazareth: Holy Week: From the Entrance into Jerusalem to the Resurrection*, London: CTS, 2011.

_____ *Sacramentum Caritatis*, 2007.

Pope Francis, *Address to the Faithful of the Diocese of Rome*, Paul VI Audience Hall, 18 September 2021.

_____ *Desiderio Desideravi*, 2022.

_____ *Evangelii Gaudium*, 2013.

_____ *Gaudete et Exsultate*, 2018.

_____ *Homily at the National Shrine of 'Ta' Pinu' in Gozo*, 2 April 2022.

_____ *Homily for the Opening of the Synodal Path*, St Peter's Basilica, Rome, 10 October 2021.

Pope John Paul II, *Christifideles Laici*, 1988.

_____ *Ecclesia de Eucharistia*, 2003.

_____ *Mane Nobiscum Domine*, 2004.

_____ *Pastores Dabo Vobis*, 1992.

_____ *Reconciliatio et Paenitentia*, 1984.

Pope Paul VI, *Evangelii Nuntiandi*, 1975.

_____ *Ordo Paenitentiae*, 1974.

_____ *Paenitemini*, 1966.

_____ *Sacram Unctione Infirmorum*, 1972.

Rahner, K., *Foundations of the Christian Faith: An Introduction to the Idea of Christianity*, trans. W.V. Dych, New York: Crossroad, 1978, 2000.

_____ 'The Theology of the Symbol' in *Theological Investigations*, Vol. 4, trans. K. Smyth, Baltimore: Helicon Press and London: Darton, Longman & Todd, 1966.

_____ *Über die Sakramente der Kirche*, Freiburg: Herder Verlag, 1985 [French edition: *Les Sacraments de l'Eglise*, trans. M. Debacker, Paris: Nouvelle cité, 1987].

Ratzinger, J., 'Eucharist and Mission', *Irish Theological Quarterly*, Vol. 65 (2000), pp. 245–64.

Revel, J.P., *Traité des Sacrements: I. Baptême et Sacramentalité*, Paris: Cerf, 2004.

Rite of Christian Initiation of Adults, Chicago: Liturgy Training Publications, 1988.

'Sacrements', in *Dictionnaire Encyclopédique du Moyen Âge*, tome II, André Vauchez (dir.), Paris: Cerf, 1997, pp. 1355–7.

Schillebeeckx, E., *Christ the Sacrament of the Encounter with God*, London: Sheed and Ward, 1963 [Dutch orig.: *Christus, Sacrament van de Godsontmoeting*, Bilthoven: H. Nelissen, 1960].

_____ *Marriage: Secular Reality and Saving Mystery*, Vol. 2, trans. N.D. Smith, London: Sheed and Ward, 1965 [Dutch orig.: *Het huwelijk: aardse werkelijkheid en heilsmysterie*, Bilthoven: Nelissen, 1963].

Spicq, C., *Lexique théologique du Nouveau Testament*, Paris: Cerf, 1991.

Sullivan, F.A., *From Apostles to Bishops: The Development of the Episcopacy in the Early Church*, New York: Newman Press, 2001.

Synod of Bishops, *For a Synodal Church: Communion, Participation, and Mission – Synod 2021–2023 Preparatory Document*, Vatican: Libreria Editrice Vaticana, 2021.

The Divine Office II, London: Collins, 1974.

The Divine Office III, London: Collins, 1974.

The Family Haggadah, New York: Mesorah Publications, 1981.

The Holy Bible: New Revised Standard Version, London: Darton, Longman & Todd, 2005.

The New American Bible (Revised Edition), New York: HarperCollins, 2012.

Thérèse de Lisieux, *Oeuvres Complètes*, Paris: Cerf et Desclée de Brouwer, 1992.

Vanhoye, A., 'Sacerdoce commun et sacerdoce ministériel', *Nouvelle Revue Théologique*, Vol. 3 (1975), pp. 193–207.

Vatican II, *Ad Gentes: Decree on the Church's Missionary Activity*, 1965.

_____ *Christus Dominus: Decree on the Pastoral Office of the Bishops in the Church*, 1965.

_____ *Dei Verbum: Dogmatic Constitution on Divine Revelation*, 1965.

_____ *Gaudium et Spes: Pastoral Constitution on the Church in the Modern World*, 1965.

_____ *Lumen Gentium: Dogmatic Constitution on the Church*, 1964.

____ *Presbyterorum Ordinis: Decree on the Ministry and Life of Priests*, 1965.

____ *Sacrosanctum Concilium: Constitution on the Sacred Liturgy*, 1963.

____ *Unitatis Redintegratio: Decree on Ecumenism*, 1964.

Vorgrimler, H., *Sacramental Theology*, trans. L.M. Maloney, Collegeville, Minnesota: Liturgical Press, 1992 [German orig.: *Sakramententheologie*, Düsseldorf: Patmos Verlag, 1987].

Walsh, L., *Sacraments of Initiation: A Theology of Life, Word, and Rite*, Chicago: Liturgy Training Publications, 2011.